Planning Your Time in Retirement

Planning Your Time in Retirement

How to Cultivate a Leisure Lifestyle to Suit Your Needs and Interests

Robert A. Stebbins

ROWMAN & LITTLEFIELD
Lanham • Boulder • New York • Toronto • Plymouth, UK

Published by Rowman & Littlefield
4501 Forbes Boulevard, Suite 200, Lanham, Maryland 20706
www.rowman.com

10 Thornbury Road, Plymouth PL6 7PP, United Kingdom

Copyright © 2013 by Rowman & Littlefield
First paperback edition 2015

All rights reserved. No part of this book may be reproduced in any form or by any electronic or mechanical means, including information storage and retrieval systems, without written permission from the publisher, except by a reviewer who may quote passages in a review.

British Library Cataloguing in Publication Information Available

Library of Congress Cataloging-in-Publication Data
The hardback edition of this book was previously catalogued by the Library of Congress as follows:

Stebbins, Robert A., 1938–
Planning your time in retirement : how to cultivate a leisure lifestyle to suit your needs and interests / Robert A. Stebbins.
pages cm
Includes bibliographical references and index.
1. Retirement—Planning. I. Title.
HQ1062.S74 2013
646.7'9—dc23
2013016994

ISBN 978-1-4422-2159-8 (cloth : alk. paper)
ISBN 978-1-4422-4870-0 (pbk : alk. paper)
ISBN 978-1-4422-2160-4 (electronic)

∞™ The paper used in this publication meets the minimum requirements of American National Standard for Information Sciences Permanence of Paper for Printed Library Materials, ANSI/NISO Z39.48-1992.

Printed in the United States of America

To Gordon Pritchard

Contents

Preface		ix
Acknowledgments		xiii
1	What's at Stake in Retirement?	1
2	Leisure for Retirees	13
3	Amateur Activities	35
4	Hobbies	61
5	Volunteering	95
6	Leisure: Casual and Project Based	111
7	Planning a Leisure Lifestyle	129
Appendix: Nature Challenge Activities (Hobbyist/Amateur)		149
Notes		153
Bibliography and Resources		161
Index		165
About the Author		169

Preface

Much of what is written about getting old has a negative feel to it, which is certainly not entirely unjustified. It is for most elderly a time of reduced income, declining vigor, failing health, social isolation, and other less-than-pleasant transformations. True, the early years of old age and retirement are usually better than the later ones. But all those years are "sunset years," in that everyone knows the sun will eventually go down, forever.

Sounds bleak, doesn't it? But it doesn't have to be that way. Within this "dark scenario" a positive existence is possible. *Positiveness* is the term for describing a style of life felt to be worthwhile, one that is substantially filled with satisfaction and fulfillment. The term also refers to the attitude of people who enjoy a positive lifestyle. One agreeable consequence of this state of mind is its capacity for assuaging, if not downright healing, life's negative thoughts and experiences. Everyone wants to be happy, but much of the discussion of this emotion, both academic and popular, is long on platitudes and description and short on usable practical advice as to how to set off in this direction.

In other words, though we all know our story will eventually come to a dark ending, it is possible to keep some welcome illumination brightly shining until that final chapter. Much of that illumination emanates from positive leisure activities. But here we must be careful about what we actually mean by the word *leisure* and the somewhat simplified image of leisure that inhabits the popular mind. That image portrays what we do in our free time as casual and carefree; as requiring little or no effort, skill, or knowledge; as being, in a word, "fun."

For some retirees, a post-work existence consisting of fun works well. They have managed to shape an interesting casual leisure lifestyle, and it will be the subject of chapter 6.

Seldom included in the popular image of leisure, however, are two other types of leisure that are also widely available to retirees. In the field of leisure studies—the scientific basis for this book—these types are known as *serious leisure* and *project-based leisure*. The first is the leisure of amateurs, hobbyists, and serious volunteers. The activities pursued by these people require significant effort, skill, and knowledge; they are not carefree pursuits, but are instead driven by a deep, long-term commitment. Project-based leisure also entails such a commitment, but usually demands much less skill or knowledge. Such projects, however, may require a considerable, albeit short-term, effort.

Let us look more particularly at these serious leisure participants—those who eschew the smorgasbord of casual activities now widely available to everyone in favor of something more substantial. They are found in the fine and entertainment arts and in science and sport. The hobbyists' world is populated by collectors and makers-of and tinkerers-with ranging from quilters to "do-it-yourselfers." Some sports and games are better considered hobbies than amateur pursuits. And under the heading of hobbies we include noncompetitive activities like hunting, orienteering, canoeing, and hiking. Finally, there are the reading hobbies. Chapters 3 and 4 cover these two kinds of serious leisure.

The third kind of serious leisure—*serious volunteering*—has its own chapter. Some retirees, as well as adults in earlier stages of life, gain a profound sense of personal fulfillment by helping out in an area that interests them greatly. Six of these interests are covered in chapter 5: popular (helping other people), idea-based (e.g., serving a religion or political party), material (e.g., preserving artifacts, historical sites), floral (e.g., tending a community garden), faunal (e.g., working in animal rescue), and environmental (e.g., cleaning up a water supply, controlling mosquitoes). Note, however, that some volunteering is essentially casual leisure, but nonetheless much appreciated by those benefiting from it. Someone has to take tickets at the door of the high school play, shovel the sidewalk leading to the church, and distribute leaflets on street corners.

Most retirees like to mix these three kinds of leisure, whether in combinations of casual and project-based activities or in combinations of serious and casual pursuits. The result is a leisure lifestyle that is tailor-made by the individual to suit that person's tastes, talents, and financial situation. And by engaging in some *positive simplicity*—application of the principles of simple living in the domain of leisure activities—many people in this stage of life can immensely enjoy the twilight that precedes the sunset. I also point out that such enjoyment is sometimes achieved by engaging in devotee work—that is, a serious leisure pursuit from which the worker derives a measure of livelihood, typically some kind of income.

Exacerbating the negative image of aging, the financial situation of the modern retiree is also the subject of considerable literature. This literature, like much of the material related to the emotion of happiness, is long on advice, though in this instance it is very practical advice about the financial ins and outs of leaving the workforce. This book makes no attempt to cover this important field. It has already been done, as is evident in the long list of books that can be found on the subject on Amazon.com by using the search phrase "retirement planning." Rather, this book centers on the panoply of available free-time activities as they relate to retirees' economic situation at their stage of life.

Thus the management of time and money is not ignored, but rather examined in a unique way through the lens of positive simplicity. Moreover, although a handful of books and websites have presented a fair range of leisure activities for retirees, none of them have encompassed and explained the enormous range of activities of serious leisure in the retirement years. Therefore, a perspective on casual leisure, project-based leisure, the serious pursuits, and the interrelationship of these three serves as the theoretic basis for the present volume.

"To retire is to begin to die," lamented Pablo Casals, by which he meant that, as a gifted cellist and conductor, he would no longer be able to pursue his two passions. This book takes an obliquely different position, arguing instead that we can find Casals-like passions *in* retirement, when none existed before. This discovery can make that period of life seem hugely positive, unless, of course, you have had a career devoted to work that you love and are forced to abandon. In fact, Casals never faced this predicament, for he died suddenly of a heart attack, still working at age ninety-seven. Nonetheless, retirement was on his mind, as it is for those who retire at fifty or seventy and must begin thinking about what to do in their free time.

Acknowledgments

My first brush with the issue of leisure in retirement dates to 1978, when I published an article on the subject in the *Journal of Physical Education and Recreation*. From that time on I have occasionally pondered just how rich one's leisure lifestyle can be in full-time retirement and how many retirees and pre-retirees seem oblivious to this pot of gold awaiting them at the end of their working years. Following an interview in 2012 with Ruth Dempsey, created for presentation on her *Aging Horizons Bulletin: A Canadian Bimonthly Educational Webzine*, we discussed the need for this book. "In such a book, you shouldn't write like an academic," she counseled. "Hire a journalist to sweeten your scholarly prose."

Alex Frazer-Harrison was that journalist, whom I thank for making the text more reader friendly. Technical terms remain, however, for they are the mental signposts that guide retirees through the maze of today's leisure activities toward a vigorous retirement lifestyle. Alex dealt with style, in which he was further assisted by Gary Hamel, copyeditor for Rowman & Littlefield. The book's production was efficiently overseen by Patricia Stevenson. Suzanne Staszak-Silva, acquisitions editor, made it all possible by arranging for the manuscript to be reviewed and then contracting me to write the following pages.

Chapter One

What's at Stake in Retirement?

> Don't simply retire from something; have something to retire to.
>
> Harry Emerson Fosdick

Retirement, the term implies, begins after work. In this book, the term refers not to getting another job, but to the life of leisure possible in the free time that is now available. We shall see, however, that some people do find paying work in retirement that is so appealing that they see it as essentially leisure. These retirees are also part of this book, as are those who find part-time work and thus still have considerably more time for leisure than when they worked full-time.

In past generations, retirement was commonly associated with a specific age—usually sixty-five—which, for the most part, was linked with legislation, eligibility to receive income-supplement benefits from the government, and eligibility to begin collecting on pensions and retirement savings. These days, people retire for more reasons than most of us can imagine or even care to contemplate. We know our own reasons and usually those of close friends and relatives, and they are complicated enough without trying to understand the joys and woes other people feel when transiting from paid employment to living without it. So the last day at work, followed by the first day in retirement, is a unique event for each of us who turns this momentous corner in life's journey. Emotions—some good, some bad—are bound to be high at this time.

You might get the impression from these words that the occasion of retirement is a sort of black-and-white affair (or is it white-and-black?), during which you are employed until quitting time, after which you receive your final paycheck and enter a new life. The transition may last no more than two or three hours, marked by a farewell party or celebratory evening. And, for some retirees, this is pretty much how it works. The next day, the new life begins and they must figure out how to lead it.

Others, however, do not go through so abrupt a transition. True, they may also be treated to an office party, walking out the door afterward, final check and gold watch in hand. But they differ from the other type of retiree in that they leave work with plans formulated for the coming months and years. Moreover, some within this second group have for many years been preparing for their post-retirement lives. For them, their existence after work is not a black-and-white affair but one of shades of gray as they make their plans and prepare for the day they leave work and move effectively and enthusiastically into a world of leisure they know well.

Let us look at three typical leisure lifestyles often followed in the years leading up to retirement day.

Mark—Regenerative Leisure

Mark holds the position of data analyst at Ajax Engineering. He puts in long hours there because, as a salaried employee, he is expected to fulfill his duties, no matter how much time it takes. After work, particularly on weekends, he economizes by completing the occasional do-it-yourself project around the house. Thus, life for Mark is filled mostly with obligations, with very little time for play. He has no hobbies. Rather, what little leisure he has comes mainly from watching television. For Mark, television is chiefly recreational, a way of regenerating himself for the obligations of the next day. His leisure offers him few benefits apart from this function.

Nancy—Diverse Casual Leisure

Nancy's job as a department manager for a large wholesale firm seldom requires her to work overtime. Moreover, since she lives alone in an apartment, the number of domestic obligations is small. Consequently, during her evenings and weekends, she is largely free to pursue her leisure of choice. Here, Nancy likes variety, but nothing too demanding. Some of the time she watches television at home alone, but, preferring to be with friends, she spends most of her leisure hours elsewhere. With them, she dines out, attends films, goes dancing, goes for walks in the park, and passes hours in various coffee houses and jazz clubs listening to the music and conversing on a wide variety of subjects. After a couple of hours, any one of these activities becomes boring, stimulating Nancy to seek something else to do. She enjoys her leisure lifestyle chiefly because of the variety it offers.

Tom and Marge—Serious Leisure

Tom and Marge are a married couple living in their own house. He is a building contractor; she teaches elementary school. Although they are homeowners, neither cares much for the usual domestic obligations routinely faced by such people. Rather than meet these obligations themselves, they either ignore them or hire someone to do them. Since both must occasionally work long hours at their jobs, they avoid wherever possible other activities that would take time away from their leisure passion: the hobby of barbershop singing. Each belongs to a chorus and a quartet, but not the same ones, since sexually mixed units are rare in this art. Performing, practicing, and rehearsing consume a great deal of after-work time each week. Marge also serves as the publicity coordinator for her chorus, though this falls outside of the hobby category and is more of a volunteer activity. Tom and Marge's leisure lifestyle is powerfully attractive, partly because it enables them to experience a number of deeply felt benefits such as self-development and self-enrichment.

Nancy and Tom and Marge will have a shades-of-gray type of transition to retirement; their leisure lifestyle is already in place. True, they will now have more free time on their hands, but having experience with how to manage it, they will probably do this effectively. However, Mark's transition is of the black-and-white variety. He must now build a leisure lifestyle, whether it be like that of Nancy, that of Tom and Marge, or something else. Or he could expand to full-time, as it were, his recreational use of his free time.

FINANCING RETIREMENT

To a certain extent, what we do in retirement depends on our financial situation. I might, once retired, want to travel the world over, but my savings and pension (should I have one) are too meager for such dreams. Nancy, Tom, and Marge may not face this problem of financially unrealistic post-work desires, because they have worked out before retirement a leisure lifestyle they can support. Nevertheless, they will have to consider the monetary implications of the new activities they take on, now that they have more time for them.

By contrast, Mark, having failed to plan for his leisure in the golden years, must now start to make some lifestyle-related decisions. His financial situation will inevitably be a consideration as he becomes acquainted with various ways to spend his newfound free time. This scenario does assume, however, that Mark will want to do this sooner or later. He could, at the start, drift into a life of ennui. An unknown, but nevertheless significant number of new retirees begin this stage of life with a diet of hedonic activities like watching television, hanging out in shopping centers and coffee shops, and sitting on park benches. Such an existence usually costs very little money, but, on the other side of the coin, it soon becomes boring. People like Mark, who have given little thought to life after work, are ripe for this unsettling situation. Consider the case of another couple, Robert and Ethel:

After twenty-five years working a stressful nine-to-five job managing a meat-packing plant, Robert finally retired, and he and his wife, Ethel, settled into long-awaited quiet retirement at their dream cabin at the lake. For the first several months, it was bliss: quiet strolls along nature trails, quiet coffees overlooking the lake, and the occasional run into town for supplies.

But soon boredom and loneliness set in. There was always the Internet, but it wasn't the same; Robert and Ethel felt isolated, cut off from family and friends and the hustle and bustle of their town, which they never even realized they would miss.

Boredom soon turned to bickering, and to conversations of little more substance than discussing the weather.

Ultimately, Robert and Ethel realized they had chosen the wrong path for their retirement and came up with a new plan. They moved back to the big city, and Robert picked up work as a part-time instructor at a community college, teaching night-class students the tricks of managing business. It was paid work, pursued part-time, but it was also interesting enough to Robert for it to be considered leisure, or, in his case, what we will discuss in the next chapter as "devotee work."

This book focuses on the uses of leisure in retirement, rather than on the ins and outs of financial planning for this period of life, recognizing as we just did that free-time activities can be costly, and the choices retirees make are explained in part by their capacity to fund those choices. It is their interest in leisure and the constraints imposed on it by limited financial resources that stir in many a retiree a complementary interest in positive simplicity. This is a critical juncture in retirement—and there may be several, depending on how many activities are considered—for the powerful appeal of leisure activities can easily outrun the capacity of one's bank account to allow for their pursuit at a satisfying level. Moreover, discretionary income for most people is lower in retirement than before and, for many, may be getting lower.[1]

Positive Simplicity

The term *positive simplicity* refers to the application of the principles of simple living in the domain of leisure activities. It is a process whereby people reduce what they come to realize are avoidable expenses and activities—a process that can be implemented anywhere, at any time, in any period of life. I will, however, concentrate on the post-retirement years. Here, simplicity is qualified by the adjective *positive*, because it is done to facilitate pursuit of personally worthwhile leisure activities. For some people, voluntary simplicity lacks this spirit, it being followed primarily to help solve a monstrous social problem such as environmental pollution, overuse of natural resources, or inferior commercial produce (a problem solved by growing your own).

In his 2010 book *Voluntary Simplicity*, Duane Elgin, who was heavily influenced by Mohandas Gandhi, writes that, among other things, it is

> a way of living that accepts the responsibility for developing our human potentials, as well as for contributing to the well-being of the world of which we are an inseparable part; a paring back of the superficial aspects of our lives so as to allow more time and energy to develop the heartfelt aspects of our lives.[2]

The voluntary simplicity movement, which also goes by the names of, among others, "simple living" and "creative simplicity," was launched in the mid-1930s with an article written by Richard Gregg (for bibliographic information on the several reprinted versions of this article, see Elgin, 297–98). The idea may be much older, however, as suggested by the following biblical citation: "Better is a handful with quietness, than both the hands full with travail and vexation of spirit" (Ecclesiastes 4:6).

Note that in pursuing either serious leisure or project-based leisure (discussed in chapter 2) participants make many contributions to the community (the "world," in the Elgin quotation). Note, too, that these two forms offer separate avenues for realizing human potential. It is, therefore, reasonable to interpret participation in such leisure as consistent with the principles of voluntary simplicity, in general, and positive simplicity, in particular. Furthermore, an interest in simple living and finding leisure do share the common ground of encouraging and fostering self-fulfillment through realizing individual human potential while also contributing to the well-being of the wider community. For the typical, true votary of voluntary simplicity, this also frequently means paring back one's work activity at times when such activity brings in more money than needed for the simple life and uses up time that could be spent in leisure activities that together are both satisfying and fulfilling.

The main idea here is to identify the road to a sound financial base for leisure founded on the principles of positive simplicity as an adjunct to the fruits of preretirement financial planning. The latter, of course, is also a good idea, but not everyone does it or has the resources with which to plan effectively. Thus BlackRock's 2011 National Retirement Survey in the United States revealed that just over half of the retirees surveyed—but only one-quarter of today's workers—are confident they will have enough money to live comfortably in retirement.[3]

Thus, some measure of positive simplicity may be unavoidable in retirement for a huge segment of the retired population, all of whom have an interest in a vibrant leisure lifestyle. After all, this is now their principal domain of life. Happily, LifeEdited.com is now available to help them along.

NONWORK OBLIGATION

That said, there is nevertheless another, third domain. It is centered on nonwork obligations, which are, by definition, disagreeable in some measure (when such obligations are *agreeable*, they are, in effect, leisure). Some of these disagreeable requirements are capable of undermining positiveness in life. By contrast, an agreeable obligation is very much a part of some leisure, evident when such obligation accompanies positive commitment to an activity that evokes pleasant memories and expectations, two essential features of leisure, says Max Kaplan.[4] Meanwhile, disagreeable obligation has no place in leisure because, among other reasons, it fails to leave the participant with a pleasant memory or expectation of the activity. Rather, it is the stuff of this third domain. It is the classificatory home of all we must do that we would rather avoid that is not related to work (including moonlighting).

So far, I have been able to identify three types of nonwork obligation.[5] Bear in mind that this typology is in its early stages of development, an initial attempt to bring some order to an area of life that seriously lacks systematic research.

Unpaid labor: activities that people do themselves, even though services exist which they could hire to carry out these tasks. These activities include mowing the lawn, housework, shoveling the sidewalk, preparing the income tax returns, do-it-yourself projects of a non-hobby variety, and a myriad of obligations to friends and family (e.g., caring for a sick relative, helping a friend move to another home, arranging a funeral).

Unpleasant tasks: required activities for which no commercial services exist or, if they exist, most people would avoid using. Such activities are exemplified in checking in and clearing security at airports, attending a meeting on a community problem, walking the dog each day, driving in city traffic (in this discussion, driving beyond that which is related to work), and running errands, including routine grocery shopping and paying bills at the bank. There are also obligations to family and friends that come under this umbrella, such as driving a child to soccer practice and mediating familial quarrels. Many of the "chores" of childhood fall into this category. Finally, activities sometimes mislabeled as volunteering are, in fact, disagreeable obligations from which the individual senses no escape. For example, some parents feel this way about coaching their children's sports teams or helping out with a road trip for the youth orchestra in which their children play.

Self-care: disagreeable activities designed to maintain or improve in some way the physical or psychological state of the individual. They include getting a haircut, putting on cosmetics, exercising, going to the dentist, and undergoing a physical examination. Personal and family counseling also fall within this type, as do the activities that accompany getting a divorce.

Some activities in these types are routine obligations, whereas others are only occasional. And, of course, for those who find some significant measure of enjoyment in, say, grocery shopping, walking the dog, do-it-yourself activities, or taking physical exercise, these obligations are actually defined as agreeable; they are, in reality, leisure. On grocery shopping, for example, the *Economist* reports data from a survey indicating that "large numbers" of the sample in fact liked shopping for food.[6] Thus, what is disagreeable in the domain of nonwork obligation depends on personal interpretation of the actual or anticipated experience. So most people dislike (or expect to dislike) their annual physical examination, but not the hypochondriac.

Another leading concern for the retiree thrown up by the domain of nonwork obligation is that it reduces further (after work is done) the amount of free time for leisure and, for some people, devotee work—that is, an occupation that they are happy to be in (which will be discussed in chapter 2). Such obligation may threaten the latter, because it may reduce the time occupational devotees, enamored as they are of their core work activities, would like to put in at work. Call this overtime, if you wish, but, as with all leisure, it has inherent attractions.

Let us turn now to the second implication of Elgin's conception of voluntary simplicity. It is that, in effecting a lifestyle truly consistent with the general tenets of voluntary simplicity, adherents of this lifestyle also appear destined both to increase their list of nonwork obligations and to reduce the amount of free time in which "heartfelt" leisure might be pursued. Consider that living simply might require a person to, for instance, walk and use public transit (in lieu of driving a car), take recyclable trash to a recycling depot (in lieu of having it collected and trucked to the municipal landfill), grow vegetables or bake bread (in lieu of buying these items at a supermarket), and acquire and use wood for home heating (in lieu of purchasing gas or oil for this purpose). Some of these simple living obligations might well be seen by some people as pleasant, as essentially leisure, including tending a garden, baking bread, and even chopping wood for home heating. But all such activities take time, which is to be found in the weekly hours of free time the individual has. When the activity is disagreeable, this robbing of Peter to pay Paul cuts into the hours that might be used for self-fulfilling free-time activities. It also cuts into time for casual leisure, consequently weakening access to, or the experience of, its several benefits (set out in chapter 2), besides leaving fewer of these activities for rounding out an optimal leisure lifestyle. What is more, people—to the extent that they are absorbed with both work and nonwork obligations—now have, when it comes to trying to organize their daily lives, significantly less room for maneuvering.

We shall return to positive simplicity from time to time throughout the remainder of this book, particularly as it pertains to particular kinds of leisure activities and to our consumptive habits as these are brought into retirement and sometimes get modified after that. But, speaking of consumption, just how does it relate to positive simplicity in the senior years?

LEISURE AND CONSUMPTION

Elsewhere, I have suggested that the end of consumption is to *have* something, to possess it for a period of time, whereas the end of leisure is to *do* something, to engage in an activity.[7] An *activity* is a type of pursuit in which participants mentally or physically (often both) think or do something, motivated by the hope of achieving a desirable goal. Life is filled with activities, both pleasant and unpleasant: sleeping, mowing the lawn, taking the train to work, having a tooth filled, eating lunch, playing tennis matches, running a meeting, and on and on. Activities, as illustrated by this list, may be categorized as work, leisure, or nonwork obligation, depending on how you look at them.

Sometimes, as in the activity of buying a ticket for an entertainment venue or paying a fee for a massage, consumption and leisure—having and doing—are virtually the same thing. I labeled this *initiatory consumption*. At other times, however, the two are separate. For example, the painter buys supplies and brushes primarily to facilitate an activity—namely, creating images on canvas. Here, the idea of having, though necessary, is only a facilitator of the powerful experience of artistic innovation. This is *facilitative consumption*.

Note, too, that many kinds of leisure activities require no significant consumption at all, among them strolling in nature, dabbling on the piano, collecting leaves or sea shells, and engaging in sociable conversation. This is *nonconsumptive leisure*. Such leisure is good news for low- and middle-income groups searching for something interesting but inexpensive to do when not faced with life's many obligations.

By trying to smother all leisure in the blanket of consumption, as some thinkers are wont to do, we neglect a wide variety of free-time activities that are both fulfilling for the individual and capable of contributing to community life—activities that are ends in themselves, even while some of them may require significant purchase of "facilitators" (e.g., a quality violin, cross-country skis, cooking ingredients, or automotive parts).[8] In summary, the significance of consumptive having in leisure, when it is a factor at all, must be judged by its role in doing the leisure activity the participant is pursuing.

Furthermore, leisure is not only doing something but also doing something *positive*. Still, its relationship to consumption is, in fact, more complicated than this. Thus, throughout this book, I consider consumptive behavior with reference to the three different forms of leisure—serious, casual, and project based—and to their types and subtypes. The practical acts of buying, say, a cup of coffee over which to talk casually with friends, or a new tennis racquet with which to play better one's favorite sport, lead to two markedly different kinds of leisure experiences. The first, which is casual leisure, could also be classified today as mass leisure, whereas the second, which is serious leisure, certainly could not. More profoundly, the second offers an avenue for self-fulfillment that is impossible to find in the first.

In short, the leisure that follows from consumption, to the extent that consumption is even necessary for that leisure, varies immensely. We sometimes need money to enable our leisure, but, oriented by positive simplicity, we might deny ourselves some initiatory consumption using the money saved to facilitate our serious activities. Voluntary simplicity and its cousin, positive simplicity, fly in the face of working and spending, both of which have been, for many years, the mantra of middle- and upper-class society in North America. To cut back on costs of housing, automotive transportation, consumer goods, and the like, in order to save money, and, with it, pursue serious leisure, is, in this part of the world, a most unusual approach to the use of free time. But the powerful appeal of serious leisure demands this of participants of modest means, among them many retirees.

It is not that retirees living on modest pensions must, to pursue a combination of satisfying and fulfilling leisure, live as paupers or perform all their nonwork obligations. Yet many in this group will engage in some positive simplicity, probably often without knowing it, showing, inadvertently, their allegiance to this principle. They do whatever it takes to facilitate the pursuit of their serious leisure passions. Just how voluntarily simple they are when it comes to buying equipment or services for their hobby is, however, another question.

Although I did not probe directly in the interviews on this matter, I did get the sense in my study of snowboarding, river kayaking, and mountain climbing that, generally, their participants buy what they need. They buy at a level of quality necessary to get them effectively and efficiently through a typical outing at their level of competence.[9] This is not being extravagant. Thus, a kayaker might own three different kinds of boats, routinely using all three according to the kind of water to be tackled and the sort of maneuvers to be undertaken on it. Moreover, they will be of sufficient quality to effectively and efficiently enable this person to get the job done. Sure, using these standards, a few will be inclined to spend more than necessary, to buy the Cadillac of kayaks, for instance, when a Ford would do just as well. I once knew a cellist in a civic orchestra, the quality of whose instrument would have aroused jealousy in many a professional orchestral musician. But he was eventually asked to leave the orchestra because he was unable to play acceptably, as judged by the group's quite tolerant standards, even the simplest music that it presented at its concerts. You may aspire to own a Cadillac, but you still need to know how to parallel park.

CONCLUSION

In principle, then, leisure is a good thing. But, in everyday life, people often have trouble finding leisure activities capable of generating the sort of deep satisfaction and fulfillment that Tom and Marge found, activities that can serve as the basis for an optimal leisure lifestyle. This chapter has shown that some of them may be expensive when measured against a retiree's pension, necessitating, possibly, some experimenting with positive simplicity.

Still, a great deal depends on the activity chosen, degree of passion for it, ease of accessibility, alternatives to it, and so on. In the next chapter, we examine the field of leisure under the heading of the serious leisure perspective. This survey will acquaint the reader with the vast array of different kinds of activities, the rewards and benefits that come from doing them, the costs they sometimes incur, and their place in the personal and social lives of participants.

Chapter Two

Leisure for Retirees

> Happiness is not something ready-made. It comes from your own actions.
> Dalai Lama

Serious, casual, and project-based leisure were mentioned from time to time in the preceding chapter. So far as we know in the interdisciplinary field of leisure studies, these three ideas together embrace all leisure activities. For people looking for something to do in retirement that is inherently attractive, it is important to know what they might choose from. What activities are available? What do they offer the participant? How much do they cost? What are their drawbacks? The remainder of this book deals with these considerations and others, while the present chapter provides an overview of the types of activities to which they pertain.

This look into the vast world of leisure and what it can offer is not only for retirees but also for people contemplating this unique status in life. Typically, people in both categories have a woefully incomplete understanding of this world. They know their own leisure, the leisure of their friends and relatives, and possibly some of the eye-catching leisure reported in the mass media, but little else. Because they have never heard of them, they are typically unaware of the appeal of the multitude of lesser-known activities like scrapbooking, amateur botany, volunteering at the zoo, and collecting pins.

Being uninformed of the array of leisure opportunities can lead to decisions such as the following for those who are closing in on retirement:

Andy Cichos always thought that, at 55, he'd kiss the working life goodbye.

However, as he got closer to retirement age, the former vice-president of external relations for Bow Valley College [a community college in Calgary, Canada] found it more and more difficult to envision life without the challenges and rewards of employment....

"The closer I got to actually retiring, the more I thought it doesn't make any sense," Cichos said.[1]

This quotation suggests that Mr. Cichos wanted to retire but had little idea of the challenging and rewarding activities that awaited him in the domain of leisure. Meanwhile, he had such activities at work, so why abandon them?

From the sound of it, Mr. Cichos has found some deeply fulfilling leisure in his work, and as such it appears to meet the description of devotee work, discussed later in this chapter. Other workers are less fortunate; their work is not as inherently attractive as devotee work is. Yet some of them stay on the job into what could be their retirement years because they are unfamiliar with the rich world of leisure they could tap into. Others remain employed because, as observed in the preceding chapter, they have insufficient income with which to retire. In all cases it is a most valuable asset to know about today's leisure opportunities beyond the superficial picture of them held in the popular mind. Such information can help us find a style of life well worth living and possibly also provide some income.

THREE TYPES OF LEISURE

As far as we know at present, all leisure may be classified as serious, casual, or project based. It will help in the discussion that follows to have a general understanding of these three.[2] Note, too, that this is only an introduction, for we will examine each much more closely later in this chapter.

The serious type comes in two varieties: serious leisure and devotee work. Because of their similarity we will occasionally refer to them together as the *serious pursuits*. *Serious leisure* is the systematic pursuit of an amateur, hobbyist, or volunteer activity. It is sufficiently substantial, interesting, and fulfilling for the participant to find a career there acquiring and expressing a combination of its special skills, knowledge, and experience. This career is experienced in free time, however, during which the individual gets better and better as an amateur, hobbyist, or volunteer. It may be necessary to persevere when, for example, mastery of a skill or idea proves elusive. And because decline is possible in these activities (e.g., athletes who are past their prime), decline may also be part of this kind of career.

Devotee work is activity in which participants feel a powerful devotion or strong, positive attachment; it is an occupation that they are proud to be in. In such work the sense of achievement is high and the core activity endowed with such intense appeal that the line between this work and leisure is virtually erased. Thus one way of understanding this level of appeal is to view devotee work as serious leisure from which a full or partial livelihood is possible.

By contrast, *casual leisure* is immediately intrinsically rewarding, relatively short-lived pleasurable activity. It requires little or no special training to enjoy it. It is therefore fundamentally hedonic, pursued for its significant level of pure enjoyment, or pleasure. Examples are legion, including watching entertainment TV, observing scenery, drinking a glass of wine, or gossiping about someone. Complexity in casual leisure increases slightly when playing a board game using dice, participating in a Hash House Harrier treasure hunt, or serving as a casual volunteer by, say, collecting bottles for the Scouts or making tea and coffee after a religious service.

Project-based leisure differs in many ways from the preceding types. It is a short-term, reasonably complicated, one-off or occasional but infrequent innovative undertaking. But, as with the others, it is carried out in free time, or time free of disagreeable obligation. Such leisure requires considerable planning, effort, and possibly some skill or knowledge, but is, for all that, neither serious leisure nor intended to develop into such. It is a leisure project when we volunteer to help out at an arts festival or sports event, remodel the basement at home, or arrange a big celebration for a fiftieth wedding anniversary, assuming that these are not recurrent activities for the participant.

In the field of leisure studies these three types and their subtypes are considered together under the heading of the serious leisure perspective. Figure 2.1 offers a diagrammatic view of their interrelationship. It may also be viewed as a sort of road map for our journey through the remainder of this book.

THE SERIOUS PURSUITS

We will begin with a closer look at serious leisure and then move on to its counterpart at work. My goal for the rest of this chapter is to present enough detail about the three types to enable readers to make "optimal" choices as

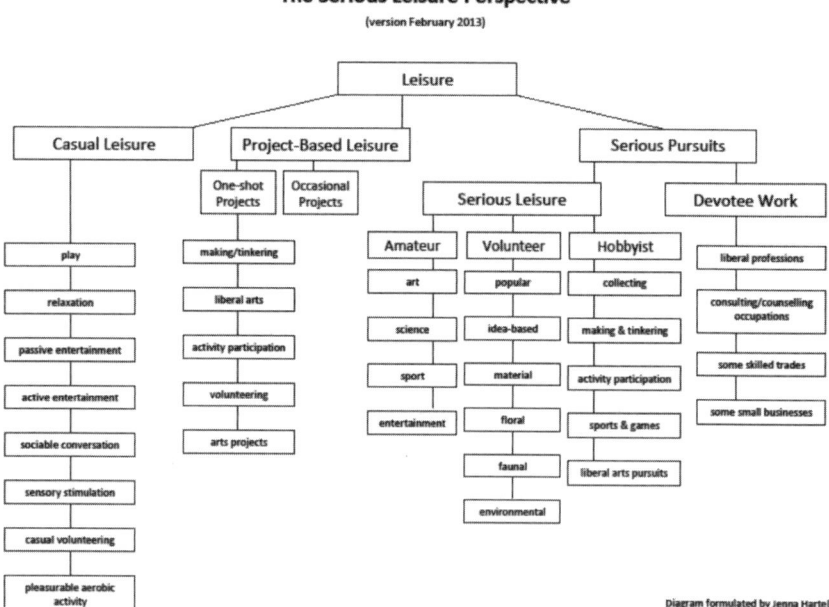

Figure 2.1.

they pursue free-time activities in retirement. Optimal choices are those leading to an exciting lifestyle in this sphere of life as experienced in a strong sense of well-being and positiveness, in a sense of self-fulfillment and possibly community contribution.

Serious Leisure

I coined the term *serious leisure* to express the way the people I interviewed and observed viewed the importance of these three kinds of activity in their daily lives.[3] The adjective *serious* (a word my research respondents often used) embodies such qualities as earnestness, sincerity, importance, and carefulness, rather than gravity, solemnity, joylessness, distress, and anxiety. Although the second set of terms occasionally describes serious leisure events, they are uncharacteristic of them and fail to nullify (or, in many cases, even dilute) the overall fulfillment gained by the participants. By way of example, an amateur actor loves performing theater, but gets stage fright before every performance.

Amateurs are found in art, science, sports, and entertainment, where they are invariably linked in a variety of ways with professional counterparts. The two can be distinguished economically in that the activity in question constitutes a livelihood (full- or part-time) for the pros but not the amateurs. The part-time professionals in art and entertainment complicate this picture; although they work part-time, their work is judged by other professionals and by the amateurs as of professional quality.

Hobbyists lack this professional alter ego, suggesting that, historically, all amateurs were hobbyists before their fields professionalized. Hobbyists can be classified in five subtypes, discussed at length in chapter 4: collectors, makers and tinkerers, noncompetitive activity participants (e.g., fishing, hiking, orienteering), sports and games hobbyists (e.g., players of ultimate Frisbee, croquet, gin rummy), and liberal arts hobbyists. The latter are enamored of the systematic acquisition of knowledge for its own sake. Many accomplish this by reading voraciously in a field of art, sport, cuisine, language, culture, history, science, philosophy, politics, or literature.

Volunteers perform, even for short periods of time, volunteer work in either an informal or a formal setting.[4] It is through volunteer work that these people provide a service or benefit to one or more individuals, usually receiving no pay, even though people serving in volunteer programs are sometimes compensated for out-of-pocket expenses. Moreover, in the field of nonprofit studies, since no volunteer work is involved, giving (of, say, blood, money, clothing), as an altruistic act, is not considered volunteering. Meanwhile, in the typical case, volunteers who are altruistically providing a service or benefit to others are themselves also benefiting from various rewards experienced during this process (e.g., pleasant social interaction, self-enriching experiences, and a sense of contributing to nonprofit group success). In other words volunteering is motivated by two basic attitudes: altruism *and* self-interest. The hobbyist and the amateur, however, are motivated significantly more by self-interest than by altruism.

The conception of volunteering that squares best with the leisure basis of this book is that volunteering is a distinctive type of leisure. Volunteers engage in enjoyable casual leisure, fulfilling serious leisure, or enjoyable or fulfilling project-based leisure doing activities that they may choose to accept or reject on their own terms. A key element in the leisure conception of volunteering is the feeling of not being coerced to participate in the volunteer activity through appeals to moral obligation or other means.[5]

Rewards, Costs, and Motivation

The main way that serious pursuits are set off from other kinds of work and leisure is by the extraordinary rewards they offer. These rewards act as powerful motives for being involved in one or more such pursuits. Still, the serious pursuits are also distinguished by the fact that participants sometimes encounter costs while engaging in them. It is this profile of rewards *and* costs that places the serious pursuits at odds with the popular images of work as drudgery and leisure as an unalloyed good time. To repeat, this is why my interviewees kept underscoring that their leisure was not like that of most other people.

The rewards of a serious leisure pursuit are the more or less routine values that attract and hold its enthusiasts. Every serious leisure career both frames and is framed by the continuous search for these rewards. Moreover, this search may take months—and in some fields, years—before the participant consistently finds self-fulfillment in his or her amateur, hobbyist, or volunteer activity. Ten rewards have so far emerged in the course of the various studies of amateurs, hobbyists, and career volunteers. As the following list shows, the first seven rewards are predominantly personal and the last three are social.

1. Personal enrichment (cherished experiences)
2. Self-actualization (developing skills, abilities, knowledge)
3. Self-expression (expressing skills, abilities, knowledge already developed)
4. Self-image (known to others as a particular kind of serious leisure participant)
5. Self-gratification (combination of superficial enjoyment and deep fulfillment)
6. Re-creation (regeneration) of oneself through serious leisure after a day's work
7. Financial return (from a serious leisure activity)
8. Social attraction (associating with other serious leisure participants, with clients as a volunteer, participating in the social world of the activity)
9. Group accomplishment (group effort in accomplishing a serious leisure project; senses of helping, being needed, being altruistic)

10. Contribution to the maintenance and development of the group (including senses of helping, being needed, being altruistic in making the contribution)

In the various studies on amateurs, hobbyists, and volunteers, these rewards, depending on the activity, were often given different weightings by the interviewees to reflect their importance relative to each other. Nonetheless, some common ground exists, for studies show that, in terms of their personal importance, most serious leisure participants rank self-enrichment and self-gratification as number one and number two. Moreover, to find either reward, participants must have acquired sufficient levels of relevant skill, knowledge, and experience and be in a position to use these acquisitions.[6] In other words, self-actualization, which was often ranked third in importance, is also highly rewarding in serious leisure.

Let me interject here a brief aside on terminology. I have in recent years taken to using the term *fulfillment*.[7] It points to a set of chronological experiences leading to the fullest development of a person's gifts and character, to development of that person's full potential. Such an acquisition is certainly both a reward and a benefit of serious leisure. Rewards 1–3 are manifestations of fulfillment.

Satisfaction, the term I used formerly, sometimes refers to a satisfying experience that is fun or enjoyable (also referred to as gratifying). In another sense this noun may refer to meeting or satisfying a need or want. In neither instance does satisfaction denote the preferred sense of fulfillment just presented. In general, satisfaction is commonly what we gain from casual leisure, whereas fulfillment typically comes with its serious counterpart. Reward 5 sometimes brings the enthusiast both, as in the jazz musician who has "fun" at a jam session (i.e., it is fun to play well while developing further as an artist).

Both rewards and costs were mentioned by research interviewees during research into their serious pursuits. More particularly, they saw their leisure as a mix of rewards offsetting costs as experienced in the central activity. Moreover, every serious pursuit contains its own combination of these costs, which each participant must confront in some way. So far, it has been impossible to develop a general list of them, as has been done for the rewards. The reason seems to be that the costs tend to be highly specific to each activity. In general terms the costs discovered to date may be classified as *disappointments*, *dislikes*, or *tensions*. Thus, it can be disappointing to fail to place in a sports contest, to not be able to afford a treasured antique for one's collection, or to lack the skill to paint a landscape as one believes it should be done. Dislikes arise in the serious pursuits when, for instance, an umpire makes what players regard as a bad call, a weekend rain spoils the backpacking trip, or a book's price discourages a hobbyist reader from purchasing it. The tensions tend to be interpersonal, as in a civic orchestra conductor who criticizes the playing of a section, friction between a volunteer coordinator and the volunteers, or disagreements with the management of a recreation center that provides racket ball and badminton courts.

Interestingly, certain positive psychological states may be founded, to some extent, on specific negative, often common, conditions (e.g., tennis elbow, frostbite [cross-country skiing], stage fright, and frustration [in acquiring a collectable, learning a theatrical part]). Such adverse conditions can enhance the senses of achievement and self-fulfillment as the enthusiast manages to conquer them. Retirees exploring a serious pursuit need to be aware of these possibilities, recognizing especially that they are normal and that many people overcome them.

Thrills and Flow

Thrills are part of this framework of rewards. They are high points, the sharply exciting events and occasions that stand out in the minds of those who pursue a kind of serious leisure or devotee work. Thrills may accompany the rewards of self-enrichment and, to a lesser extent, self-actualization and self-expression. That is, thrills in serious leisure and devotee work may be seen as situated manifestations of certain more abstract rewards; they are what participants in some fields seek as concrete expressions of the rewards they find there. They are important in large part because they motivate the participant to stick with the pursuit in the hope of finding similar experiences again and because they demonstrate that diligence and commitment can pay off. Because thrills, as defined here, are based on a certain level of mastery of an activity, they know no equivalent in casual leisure. The thrill of a roller coaster ride is qualitatively different from that of a successful descent down roaring rapids in a kayak, because the kayaker must use experience, knowledge, and skill.

The kayaker's thrill rests on what Mihalyi Csikszentmihalyi calls the *flow* experience.[8] Csikszentmihalyi holds that the sensation of flow comes with actually enacting intrinsically rewarding activity. Over the years he has identified and explored eight components of this experience:

1. sense of competence in executing the activity
2. requirement of concentration
3. clarity of goals of the activity
4. immediate feedback from the activity
5. sense of deep, focused involvement in the activity
6. sense of control in completing the activity
7. loss of self-consciousness during the activity
8. sense of time is truncated during the activity

These components are self-evident, except possibly for the first and the sixth. With reference to the first, flow fails to develop when the activity is either too easy or too difficult. To experience flow the participant must feel capable of performing what that person regards as a moderately challenging activity. The sixth component refers to the perceived degree of control the participant has over execution of the activity. This is not a matter of personal competence, but rather one of degree of maneuverability in confronting uncontrollable external forces. This component was well illustrated in a study of mountain hobbyists caught in a thunderstorm, kayakers paddling a suddenly rising water level on a river, and snowboarders negotiating an unpredicted snowstorm on a backcountry slope.[9]

Viewed through the prism of the serious pursuits, psychological flow tends to be associated with the rewards of self-enrichment and, to a lesser extent, those of self-actualization and self-expression. Although many types of work and leisure generate little or no flow for their participants, those that do are found primarily in the serious pursuits of devotee work and serious leisure. Still, it appears that each pursuit capable of producing flow does so in terms unique to it.

Devotee Work

Nearly all of what was just said about serious leisure also applies to devotee work. The chief difference is that the second is not carried out in free time. That is, it contributes significantly to the worker's livelihood.

Occupational devotees turn up chiefly, though not exclusively, in four areas of the economy. Further, devotee work in these areas is, at most, only lightly bureaucratized. Therefore it is most common in certain small businesses, the skilled trades, the consulting and counseling occupations, and the public- and client-centered professions. Public-centered professionals serve in the arts, sports, science, and entertainment fields, while those that are client-centered abound in such callings as law, teaching, accounting, and medicine.[10] It is assumed in all this that the work and the core activity to which people become devoted carry a respectable identity vis-à-vis their reference groups. It would be difficult, if not impossible, to be devoted to work that those groups regarded with scorn. Still, positive identification with the job is not a defining condition of occupational devotion. Such identification can develop for other reasons, including a high salary, a prestigious employer, and advanced educational qualifications.

The fact that some people have careers in devotee work, and that others have the possibility to, signals that work, as one of life's domains, can be highly positive. Granted, most workers are not fortunate enough to find such work. For those who do find it, however, the work meets six criteria,[11] as explicated below:

1. The valued core activity must be profound; to perform it, acceptability requires substantial skill, knowledge, or experience or a combination of two or three of these.
2. The core activities must offer significant variety.
3. The core must also offer significant opportunity for creative or innovative work, as a valued expression of individual personality. The adjectives *creative* and *innovative* stress that the undertaking results in something new or different, showing imagination and application of routine skill or knowledge. That is, boredom is likely to develop only after the onset of fatigue experienced from long hours on the job, a point at which significant creativity and innovation are no longer possible.
4. The would-be devotee must have reasonable control over the amount and disposition of time put into the occupation (the value of freedom of action), such that he can prevent it from becoming a burden. Medium and large bureaucracies have tended to subvert this criterion, for, in the interest of the survival and development of their organization, managers have felt they must deny their nonunionized employees this freedom and force them to accept stiff deadlines and heavy workloads. But no activity, be it leisure or work, is so appealing that it invites unlimited participation during all waking hours.
5. The would-be devotee must have both an aptitude and a taste for the work in question. This is, in part, a case of one man's meat being another man's poison. John finds great fulfillment in being a physi-

cian, an occupation that holds little appeal for Jane. Meanwhile, she adores being a lawyer (work John finds unappealing).
6. The devotees must work in a physical and social milieu that encourages them to pursue often and without significant constraint the core activities. This includes avoidance of excessive paperwork, caseloads, class sizes, market demands, and the like.

Sounds ideal, if not idealistic, but in fact occupations and work roles exist that meet these criteria. In today's climate of occupational de-skilling, over-bureaucratization, and similar impediments to fulfilling core activity at work, many people find it difficult to locate or arrange devotee employment.

CASUAL LEISURE

I coined the term *casual leisure* in 1982 as part of my initial statement about serious leisure.[12] At the time, I thought the casual counterpart encompassed all activity that could not be described as serious. How shortsighted that observation was will become evident in the next section on project-based leisure.

Casual leisure is considerably less substantial than serious leisure, and offers no career of the sort found in the latter. Its types—there are eight (refer to figure 2.1)—include the following:

- *play* (e.g., daydreaming, dabbling at an activity, fiddling with something)
- *relaxation* (e.g., idling, napping, strolling, sitting, lounging, suntanning)
- *passive entertainment* (e.g., popular TV, pleasurable reading, mass market recorded music)
- *active entertainment* (e.g., games of chance, party games)
- *sociable conversation* (e.g., gossiping, joking, talking about the weather)
- *sensory stimulation* (e.g., sex, eating, drinking alcohol, sightseeing)
- *casual volunteering* (e.g., handing out leaflets, stuffing envelopes, and collecting money door-to-door—as opposed to serious leisure or career volunteering)
- *pleasurable aerobic activity* (discussed below)

The last and newest type of casual leisure to be identified—pleasurable aerobic activity—refers to physical activities requiring effort sufficient to cause marked increase in respiration and heart rate.[13] As applied here, the term *aerobic activity* is broad in scope. It encompasses all activity that calls for such effort. This, to be sure, includes the routines pursued collectively in (narrowly conceived of) aerobics classes and those pursued individually by way of televised or videotaped programs of aerobics. Yet, as with its passive and active cousins in entertainment, pleasurable aerobic activity is basically casual leisure. That is, to do such activity requires little more than minimal skill, knowledge, or experience. Examples include the game of the Hash House Harriers (a type of outdoor treasure hunt),[14] kickball (a cross between soccer and baseball),[15] "exergames" for children (a video game played on a dance floor),[16] and such children's pastimes as hide-and-seek.

Note that people may dabble (as play) in the same kinds of activities pursued seriously by amateurs, hobbyists, and career volunteers. Being unaware of this difference, some writers (e.g., *The Cult of the Amateur* by Andrew Keen, 2007) have labeled as "amateurish" all amateur activity, an assessment that the foregoing pages show is ill founded.

People seem to pursue the different types of casual leisure in combinations of two and three at least as often as they pursue them separately. For instance, every type can be relaxing, producing in this fashion play-relaxation, passive entertainment–relaxation, and so on. Various combinations of play and sensory stimulation are also possible, as in experimenting (in deviant or nondeviant ways) with drug use, sexual activity, and thrill seeking through movement. Additionally, sociable conversation accompanies some sessions of sensory stimulation (e.g., recreational drug use, curiosity seeking, displays of beauty, etc.) as well as some sessions of relaxation and active and passive entertainment (though in the latter two such conversation normally tends to be rather truncated).

This brief review of the types of casual leisure shows in detail the essential hedonism in this type of leisure. All produce a significant level of pure pleasure, or enjoyment, for their modern-day sybarites. In broad colloquial language, *casual leisure* could serve as the scientific term for the practice of doing what comes naturally. Yet, paradoxically, this leisure is by no means wholly frivolous, for we shall see shortly that besides the evanescent hedonic enjoyment of casual leisure, it also has substantial benefits that are enduring.

It follows that terms like *pleasure* and *enjoyment* are the more appropriate descriptors of the rewards of casual leisure. The two stand in contrast to *fulfillment* and *reward*, which best describe the benefits gained in serious leisure. At least the serious leisure participants that I have interviewed over the years were inclined to describe their involvements as fulfilling or rewarding rather than pleasurable or enjoyable. Still, overlap exists, for both casual and serious leisure offer the hedonic reward of self-gratification (see reward 5). Sometimes a serious activity is also "fun" to do, though rarely is its fun aspect the main reason for doing it, which is the motive for much of casual leisure.

Benefits of Casual Leisure

Notwithstanding its hedonic nature, casual leisure is by no means wholly inconsequential, for some clear costs and enduring benefits accrue from pursuing it. I have so far been able to identify six benefits, or outcomes, of casual leisure. But since this is a preliminary list—my first attempt at developing one—it is certainly possible that future research and theorizing could add to it.[17]

One lasting benefit of casual leisure is the creativity and discovery it sometimes engenders. Serendipity is "the quintessential form of informal experimentation, accidental discovery, and spontaneous invention."[18] It usually underlies these two processes, suggesting that serendipity and casual leisure are at times closely aligned. In casual leisure, as elsewhere, serendipity can lead to highly varied results. These include a new understanding of a home gadget or government policy, a sudden realization that a particular plant or bird exists in the neighborhood, or a different way of making artistic sounds on a musical instrument. Such creativity or discovery is unintended, however, and is therefore accidental. Moreover, in casual leisure it is not ordinarily the result of an interest in trying to solve a problem, since most of the time people enjoying this kind of activity are not motivated thus. Usually problems for which solutions must be found emerge at work, while meeting nonwork obligations, or during serious leisure.

Another benefit springs from what has come to be known as *edutainment*, a portmanteau word coined in 1975 by Christopher Daniels.[19] His term joins *education* and *entertainment* in reference to another benefit of casual leisure, one that comes with participating in such mass entertainment as watching films and television programs, listening to popular music, and reading popular books and articles. Theme parks and museums are also considered sources of edutainment. While consuming media or frequenting places of this sort, these participants inadvertently learn something of substance about the social and physical world in which they live. They are, in a word, entertained and educated in the same breath. Pleasurable historical novels provide some edutainment for the reading set.

Third, casual leisure affords regeneration, or re-creation, possibly even more so than its counterpart, serious leisure, since the latter can sometimes be intense. Of course, many a leisure studies specialist has observed that leisure in general affords relaxation or entertainment, if not both, and that these constitute two of its principal benefits. What is new, then, in the observation just made is that it distinguishes between casual and serious leisure. And more importantly, the emphasis is placed on the enduring effects of relaxation and entertainment when they help enhance overall equanimity, doing so most notably in the interstices between periods of intense activity.

Still, apropos of relaxation, it is sometimes difficult to separate casual and serious leisure. Consider as an example the personal use of such systems as yoga and tai chi. Among their principal goals are enabling and encouraging participants to meditate. One by-product of such meditation is relaxation. But first the novice must learn the various moves and positions as well as the philosophy behind them. This indicates that these systems, even though their goal is relaxation, are complex enough to be considered hobbies. They are therefore serious leisure.

A fourth benefit that may flow from participation in casual leisure originates in the development and maintenance of interpersonal relationships. One of its types, the sociable conversation, is particularly fecund in this regard. But other types, when shared, as sometimes happens during sensory stimulation and passive and active entertainment, can also have the same effect. The interpersonal relationships in question are many and varied. They include those that form between friends, spouses, and members of families. Such relationships can foster personal psychological growth by promoting new shared interests. And during this process new positive appraisals of oneself may become possible.[20]

Furthermore, some forms of casual and serious leisure offer the reward of *social attraction*, or the appeal of being with other people while participating in a common activity. Nevertheless, even though some casual and serious leisure participants share certain rewards, further research on this question will likely show that these two types experience them in sharply different ways. For instance, consider the social attraction of belonging to a barbershop chorus or a company of actors. Their members engage in a great deal of specialized shoptalk, which they dearly like. Such talk differs dramatically from that of a group of people playing a party game or enjoying a boat tour. Shoptalk is highly unlikely to occur in these latter gatherings.

Well-being is still another benefit that can flow from participating in casual leisure. Speaking only for the realm of leisure, perhaps the greatest sense of well-being is achieved when a person develops an *optimal leisure lifestyle*. Such a lifestyle is "the deeply satisfying pursuit during free time of one or more substantial, absorbing forms of serious leisure, complemented by a judicious amount of casual leisure."[21] People find optimal leisure lifestyles by partaking of leisure activities that both individually and in combination realize human potential and enhance quality of life and well-being. In addition, project-based leisure, to be discussed shortly, can likewise enhance a person's leisure lifestyle. The previously mentioned study of kayakers, snowboarders, and mountain and ice climbers revealed that the vast majority of the three samples used various forms of casual leisure to optimally round out their use of free time. For them, their serious leisure was a central life interest. Nonetheless, their casual leisure contributed to their overall well-being. It allowed for relaxation, regeneration, sociability, entertainment, and other activities less intense than their serious leisure.

Still, well-being experienced during free time is more than this, for this kind of leisure, say Hutchinson and Kleiber, can contribute to self-protection through buffering stress and sustaining coping efforts.[22] Casual leisure can also preserve or restore a sense of self. This was sometimes achieved in their samples when their respondents rediscovered in casual leisure fundamental personal or familial values or a view of themselves as caring people.

Costs

As with serious leisure the casual type has its costs, albeit with one exception, not always the same ones. Some arise because the potential benefits of casual leisure have not been realized. We have so far been able to confirm five costs.

One is boredom, an unmistakable sign of momentary absence of well-being, or momentary presence of low quality of life. Boredom seems most likely to appear when the participant experiences none of the aforementioned benefits and therefore becomes disinterested in both the amount and kind of casual leisure at the moment. Weariness and restlessness are bound to follow. Still, boredom is no ineluctable feature of casual leisure, as its place in an optimal leisure lifestyle clearly illustrates. Rather, it is a possible situational condition lurking in the background, ready to spring out and spoil the person's fun should the latter somehow lose appeal.

Second, casual leisure is, in most instances, unlikely to produce for its enthusiasts a distinctive leisure identity. Few people are inclined to proclaim to the world that they are, for example, inveterate nappers, television watchers, or consumers of fast food. To the extent that faceless casual leisure dominates the free time of people, this less-than-optimal balance of leisure activities deprives them of one or more leisure identities that they could otherwise have. For instance, Ken Roberts, after analyzing the literature in the area, concluded, notwithstanding arguments to the contrary, that today's evanescent youth scenes fail to offer special identities to those who frequent them.[23] Leisure of the kind found in these scenes can enhance self-confidence and help foster positive self-images, but it is too superficial and transient to generate a special identity.

This situation also suggests a third cost: large blocks of casual leisure, even if not boring, leave little time for serious leisure and therefore in yet another way deprive the person of an optimal leisure lifestyle. Also at issue here is a significant reduction in, or at least significant barrier to, well-being and quality of life. Exclusive or nearly exclusive pursuit of pure pleasure, or hedonism, may bring a certain level of happiness, but it can never bring the richest expression of that emotion. German philosopher Arthur Schopenhauer commented on at least two occasions about happiness, boredom, and casual leisure. On one of them he observed that "the most general survey shows us that the two foes of human happiness are pain and boredom" (from "Personality; or, What a Man Is"). Later he noted that "there is no more mistaken path to happiness than worldliness, revelry, high life" (from "Our Relations with Ourselves").

A fourth cost of casual leisure is that, most often, it makes only a limited contribution to self and community. Unless the person has created, discovered, or learned something new, casual leisure is unlikely to produce a distinctive identity, which constitutes one aspect of this cost. Others aspects include the common failure of casual leisure to generate good feelings about oneself—the value of self-esteem—and to lead to self-development—the value of personal improvement. Further, much of casual leisure, outside its oftentimes considerable economic punch, otherwise contributes little to the development of the community. Development in this sense means participation by community members in an activity resulting in improvement of one or more of its identifiable aspects and strengthening communal patterns of human and institutional interrelationships.[24] Of note, however, are casual leisure volunteers; they are exceptions to the observations just made. Their work does contribute to self and community.[25]

The fifth cost, one shared with the serious pursuits, is the occasional disappointment encountered in some casual activities. How often have we gone to the cinema or a music performance and left, perhaps before it ended, deeply disappointed? Or the scenery we paid a fancy price to see cannot be viewed because of inclement weather. Or the lively conversation you hoped to have with colleagues after work turns into a bitching session about a superior you like. We expect disappointments in life, but just the same, they tarnish its rewards and benefits. Even hedonic casual leisure is not immune to such unpleasantness.

PROJECT-BASED LEISURE

Project-based leisure is the third type of leisure activity and the one most recently to join the other two.[26] It is a short-term, reasonably complicated one-off or occasional, though infrequent, creative undertaking carried out in free time, or time free of disagreeable obligation. Such leisure requires considerable planning, effort, and sometimes skill or knowledge. Yet it is neither serious leisure nor intended to develop into such. The adjective *occasional* describes widely spaced undertakings for such regular occasions as religious festivals, someone's birthday, or a national holiday. Volunteering for a sports event may be seen as an occasional project. The adjective *creative* stresses that the undertaking results in something new or different, by showing imagination and perhaps routine skill or knowledge. Though most projects would appear to be continuously pursued until completed, it is conceivable that some might be interrupted for several weeks, months, or even years. For example, a stone wall in the back garden that gets finished only after its builder recovers from an operation on his strained back. Merely a rudimentary social world springs up around the typical project. Nonetheless, it does in its own way bring together friends, neighbors, or relatives (e.g., through a genealogical project or Christmas celebration). Or it may draw the individual participant into an organizational setting, as happens when volunteering for a sports event or major convention.

Moreover, it appears that in some instances project-based leisure springs from a sense of obligation to undertake it. If so, it is nonetheless done as leisure, as uncoerced activity, in the sense that the obligation is in fact "agreeable"—the project creator in executing the project anticipates finding fulfillment, obligated or not. And worth exploring, given that some obligations can be pleasant and attractive, is the nature and extent of leisure-like projects carried out as part of paid employment. Furthermore, this discussion jibes with the additional criterion that the project, to qualify as project-based leisure, must be *seen by the project creator* as fundamentally uncoerced, fulfilling activity. Finally, note that project-based leisure cannot, by definition, refer to projects executed as part of a person's serious leisure. Examples include having a star night as an amateur astronomer or a model train display as a collector.

Though not serious leisure, project-based leisure is enough like it to justify using the serious leisure perspective to develop a parallel framework for exploring this class of activities. A primary difference is that project-based leisure fails to imbue participants with a sense of career. Otherwise, however, it is necessary to persevere; to acquire, in some cases, certain skills or knowledge; and, invariably, to put out some effort. Also present are recognizable benefits, a special identity, and often a social world of sorts—even though the latter, it appears, is usually less complicated than those in which most serious leisure activities are framed. And it may happen at times that, even when not intended at the moment as participation in a type of serious leisure, the skilled, artistic, or intellectual aspects of the project prove highly attractive. Realizing this, the participant decides after the fact to make a leisure career of the activity as a hobbyist or amateur pursuit.

Project-based leisure is also capable of generating many of the rewards experienced in serious leisure. And just as they do in serious leisure, these rewards constitute part of the motivational basis for engaging in such highly fulfilling activity. Furthermore, motivation to undertake a leisure project may have an organizational base, much as many other forms of leisure do.[27] My observations suggest that small groups, grassroots associations (volunteer groups with few or no paid staff), and volunteer organizations (paid-staff groups using volunteer help) are the most common types of organizations in which people undertake project-based leisure.

Motivationally speaking, project-based leisure may be attractive in substantial part because it, unlike serious leisure, rarely demands long-term commitment. Even occasional projects carry with them the sense that the undertaking in question has a definite end. Indeed, it may even be terminated prematurely. Thus project-based leisure is not what Robert Dubin calls a "central life interest."[28] Rather, it is viewed by participants as fulfilling (as distinguished from enjoyable or hedonic) activity that can be experienced comparatively quickly, though certainly not as quickly as casual leisure.

Project-based leisure fits into a leisure lifestyle in its own peculiar way as interstitial activity. In this it resembles some casual leisure but not most serious leisure. Project-based leisure can therefore help shape a person's optimal leisure lifestyle. For instance, it can often be pursued at times convenient for the participant. It follows that project-based leisure is nicely suited to people who, out of proclivity or extensive nonleisure obligations or both, reject serious leisure and yet also have no appetite for a steady diet of casual leisure. Among the candidates for project-based leisure are people with heavy workloads; homemakers, mothers, and fathers with extensive domestic responsibilities; unemployed individuals who, though looking for work, still have time at the moment for (I suspect, mostly one-shot) projects; and avid serious leisure enthusiasts who want a temporary change in their leisure lifestyle. Retired people who often do have time for discretionary activity may find project-based leisure attractive as a way of adding spice and variety to their lifestyles. Beyond these special categories of participant, project-based leisure offers a form of substantial leisure to all adults, adolescents, and even children looking for something interesting and exciting to do in free time that is neither casual nor serious leisure.

Types of Project-Based Leisure

It was noted in the definition just presented that project-based leisure is not all the same. Whereas systematic exploration may reveal others, two types are evident at this time: one-shot projects and occasional projects. These are presented next using the classificatory framework for amateur, hobbyist, and volunteer activities developed earlier in this chapter.

One-Shot Projects

In all these projects people generally use the talents and knowledge they have at hand, even though for some projects they may seek certain instructions beforehand, including reading a book or taking a short course. And some projects resembling hobbyist activity participation may require a modicum of preliminary conditioning. Always, the goal is to undertake successfully the one-off project and nothing more, and sometimes a small amount of background preparation is necessary for this. It is possible that a survey would show that most project-based leisure is hobbyist in character and the next most common, a kind of volunteering. First, the following hobbyist-like projects have so far been identified, with those in the areas of making and tinkering, the liberal arts, and the arts often requiring some background utilitarian reading:

Making and tinkering:

- Interlacing, interlocking, and knot-making from kits
- Other kit assembly projects (e.g., stereo tuner, craft store projects)
- Do-it-yourself projects done primarily for fulfillment, some of which may even be undertaken with minimal skill and knowledge (e.g., build a rock wall or a fence, finish a room in the basement, or plant a special garden); this could turn into an irregular series of such projects, spread out over many years, possibly even transforming the participant into a hobbyist

Liberal arts:

- Family history (not as ongoing hobby): genealogy, scrapbooking, memory journaling
- Tourism: special trip, not as part of an extensive personal tour program, to visit different parts of a region, a continent, or much of the world
- Renaissance-man reading projects (e.g., read all the Pulitzer Prize winners in letters and drama for a particular year or set of years)

Activity participation:

- long backpacking trip, canoe trip; one-off mountain ascent (e.g., Fuji, Rainier, Kilimanjaro)

One-off volunteering projects are also common, though possibly somewhat less so than hobbyist-like projects. And less common than either are the amateur-like projects, which seem to concentrate in the sphere of theater.

Volunteering:

- Volunteer at a convention or conference, whether local, national, or international in scope

- Volunteer at a sporting competition, whether local, national, or international in scope
- Volunteer at an arts festival or special exhibition held in a museum
- Volunteer to help in restoring human life or wildlife after a natural or human-made disaster caused by, for instance, a hurricane, earthquake, oil spill, or industrial accident

Arts projects:

- Entertainment theater: produce a skit or one-off community pageant; prepare a home film, video, or set of photos
- Public speaking: prepare a talk for a reunion, an after-dinner speech, an oral position statement on an issue to be discussed at a community meeting
- Memoirs: therapeutic audio, visual, and written productions by the elderly; life histories and autobiographies (all ages); accounts of personal events (all ages)

Occasional Projects

The occasional projects seem more likely to originate in or be motivated by agreeable obligation than their one-off cousins. Examples of occasional projects include the sum of the culinary, decorative, or other creative activities undertaken, for example, at home or at work for a religious occasion or someone's birthday. Likewise, national holidays and similar celebrations sometimes inspire individuals to mount occasional projects consisting of an ensemble of inventive elements.

Unlike one-off projects, occasional projects have the potential to become routinized, which happens when new creative possibilities no longer come to mind as the participant arrives at a fulfilling formula wanting no further modification. North Americans who decorate their homes the same way each Christmas season exemplify this situation. Indeed, it can happen that, over the years, such projects may lose their appeal, but not their necessity. Thus they turn into disagreeable obligations, with their creators no longer defining them as leisure.

And, lest it be overlooked, note that one-off projects also hold the possibility of becoming unpleasant. Thus, the hobbyist genealogist gets overwhelmed with the details of family history and the challenge of verifying dates. The thought of putting in time and effort doing something once considered leisure but which she now dislikes makes no sense. Likewise, volunteering for a project may turn sour. The volunteer is now faced with a disagreeable obligation, which, however, must still be honored. This is leisure no more.

CONCLUSION

I have to this point in the present chapter intentionally avoided the subject of positive simplicity. Instead, my aim has been to paint a broad portrait of today's leisure opportunities and in this way move beyond their image in the popular mind. The lifestyle changes that may be needed, including in some instances monetary outlay, are important considerations when pondering these opportunities. Still, those considerations are best dealt with as they bear on particular activities. To try to cram them into the foregoing "big picture" would have seriously cluttered the canvas. The portrayal would have become too busy, with the result that the sense of the comprehensive scope and multifarious value of leisure and its types and subtypes would have been lost.

In the coming chapters, however, positive simplicity will return, appearing as an omnipresent leitmotif. Even for leisure activities that will be described as "nonconsumptive," many retirees will want to find simple ways to most effectively pursue them. This will in some instances require changes in lifestyle, even where money is no issue.

Chapter Three

Amateur Activities

> Vocations which we wanted to pursue, but didn't, bleed, like colors, on the whole of our existence.
>
> Honoré de Balzac

Balzac was referring as much to avocations as he was to vocations. Indeed, one definition of the latter, served up in the *Oxford English Dictionary*, regards the two as the same: "The work or function to which a person is called; a mode of life or employment regarded as requiring dedication." All the serious pursuits are, by this definition, vocations, as they are also avocations. They require dedication, though the preceding chapter revealed that they also require such additional qualities as effort and perseverance along with skill, knowledge, and experience.

Our epigraph also speaks to opportunities missed. In the language of this book, it speaks to a failure to find personal fulfillment in an activity for which we have a taste and an aptitude and with which we can build on our own gifts of character. Balzac is pointing out further that we may well recognize this failure with considerable regret. How often have you heard someone lament that "if only I had stuck with [tennis, painting, wood-working, volunteering with children, etc.], I would be so much happier today."

For those who see it this way, retirement offers the last chance to recover this kind of lost ground. For others, retirement is the time to find such ground in the first place. This chapter and the next two lay out a huge range of activities by which this may be accomplished. For this second group, it is important to have as broad a selection as possible from which to choose, to be able to consider a decent sample of personally fulfilling activities. The order of presentation follows that of chapter 2. We therefore turn first to the artistic activities pursued under the heading of the fine and entertainment arts.

THE FINE AND ENTERTAINMENT ARTS

The fine arts appeal to the mind and to our sense of beauty. Many artistic works also convey a powerful social or emotional message such as ethnic injustice, national treason, or personal ruin. By comparison, most entertainment rests on pure humor or, more broadly, pure amusement. It is easily understood material intentionally designed to avoid arousing our intellect or piquing our conscience, as the fine arts sometimes do. Nevertheless, the relationship between these two fields is complex, which is why we are considering them in the same section of this book.

Part of this relationship rests on the twin facts that both fields are arts and both share many techniques. For the most part these techniques originated in the fine arts and then flowed from there to the entertainment world. Today a properly trained rock trumpeter will have received lessons in classical trumpet, giving this artist a solid base for making music as an entertainer. A person planning a career in Broadway theater learns the same fundamentals as the person planning a career on the Shakespearian stage. Nevertheless, exceptions do exist. Such theatrical skills as juggling, ventriloquism, and prestidigitation were born as entertainment techniques, and these techniques have not found broad acceptance in fine art drama (at least so far). In fact, these latter skills are more accurately seen as specialized acquisitions performed by using fundamental acting skills, among them eye contact, voice projection, and vocal enunciation.

The general sharing of basic techniques by the fine arts and entertainment fields indicates that both are skilled pursuits; to do either well requires considerable practice. Moreover, according to the definition of art set out by Thomas Munro, both are artistic because both incorporate one or more of the following skills:

1. Making or doing something used or intended for use as a stimulus for a satisfactory aesthetic experience. Aspects of this experience may include beauty, pleasantness, interest, and emotion.
2. Expressing and communicating past emotional and other experience, both individual and social.

3. Designing, composing, and performing through personal interpretation, as distinguished from routine execution or mechanical reproduction.[1]

For example, the artistic part of stand-up comedy is making people laugh, and when this happens, the art meets Munro's three criteria. It takes skill to write comic lines seen by the audience as pleasant, interesting, and emotional (i.e., humorous), or a combination of all three. It takes skill to communicate through humor one's past experiences, whether emotional or not. Finally, it takes skill to perform lines that generate laughter. On the other hand, the Shakespearian actor does not write his or her lines and is presenting drama more often than humor.

These examples illustrate the fact that fine art and entertainment have different artistic goals and consequently draw on different combinations of the three skills to produce their distinctive artistry. Note further that, although intended by their producers to be beautiful or entertaining, some objects and productions still fall short of this goal. We have all seen or heard poor-quality art and entertainment at one time or another; it is poor because it fails to meet at least one of Munro's three criteria.

Since both the entertainment and the fine arts fields evince considerable skill and artistry when done well, the common tendency to hold the second in greater esteem than the first must be kept in perspective. From what has been said here, it is evident that such ranking is tenable only on evaluative grounds: influential segments of modern society accord higher value to the pursuit of beauty and intellectual expression than to the pursuit of humor and amusement. Nonetheless, people from all levels of society enjoy being entertained and many like entertaining others. Thus many interesting work/leisure careers in both the fine arts and the entertainment fields await amateur enthusiasts from every walk of life.

The large majority of the fine arts have amateur and professional wings. They are found in the following:

Music

- jazz (vocal, instrumental)
- choral singing
- operatic singing
- chamber music
- orchestral music

Dance

- ballet
- modern

Theater

- experimental community
- classical community
- art pantomime
- art cinematic production

Art

- photography (landscapes, still life, portraits, wildlife in color or black and white)
- painting (landscapes, still life, portraits, wildlife using watercolors or oils)
- drawing (landscapes, still life, portraits, wildlife using pencil, ink, or charcoal)
- printing (stenciling, lettering, calligraphy)
- printmaking (relief, intaglio, lithography, serigraphy)
- sculpting and carving (clay, wood, metal, wire, putty)

Literature

- fiction (novels, short stories)
- poetry
- nonfiction (factual, historical, biographical books and articles)

Some of these forms need a brief explanation. Chamber music is played with one instrument or a small group of them. Consequently, it includes such solo instrumentalists as pianists, guitarists, and accordionists. Modern dance is an experimental form; it diverges radically from ballet in its emphasis on the expressiveness of the human body presented in aesthetically pleasing movements. Community theater is the theater of amateurs, enhanced at times by a featured professional principal. Although primarily classical, it does have its experimental side as well.

Entertainment is so diverse as to be nearly impossible to classify. Still, one way to try to bring some order to this chaos is to categorize the entertainment arts along the lines of their fine arts counterparts—a reasonable approach since the two types spring from the same basic techniques. The following list of entertainment arts is incomplete, since it contains only those with professional wings holding great appeal for amateurs. In the next chapter we cover several fields where professionals have yet to emerge in significant numbers.

Music

- rock music and other jazz derivatives
- country music
- folk music (commercial)

Dance

- jazz dance
- choral or show dance
- ballroom dancing
- tap dancing
- country and western
- line dancing

Theater

- commercial community (musical, operetta, comedy, drama)
- entertainment pantomime
- entertainment magic
- commercial cinematic production (home film and video) stand-up comedy
- variety arts (juggling, clowning, ventriloquism, acrobatics)
- sketch
- puppetry
- public speaking

Art

- sculpting and carving (with clay, wood, wire, metal, putty, balloons)
- drawing cartoons, caricatures

- photography (color, black-and-white)
- painting (oils, water colors)
- sketching

Literature

- fiction (novels, short stories)
- poetry
- nonfiction (factual, historical, biographical books and articles)

Here, too, some of these arts need further explanation. The folk music in this list is of the entertainment variety presented in colorful urban venues rather than the native or backcountry art found in certain isolated areas of North America and societies outside the West. Show dancing is the art of the dance choruses, which have livened up many a Broadway show.

Amateurs abound in the arts and entertainment fields. This imbalance is due in no small part to the difficulty of finding work in them that is sufficiently remunerative to sustain a half-decent living. What is more, such a living may only be possible when combined with steady part-time employment in another occupation. The stereotype of the musician–taxi driver is at least a half-truth. And then there is the joke about the musicologist (someone who studies the history and forms of music):

Question: "What do you do if a musicologist knocks at your door?"

Answer: "Pay him and take the pizza."

The enormous appeal of performing an entertainment or fine art in an era when the job market is withering away in the arid climate of the Information Age opens wide the gates of these fields to amateur participation.[2]

Effort

All the arts, if they are to be even moderately well executed, demand a certain routine effort from their practitioners. The routine is different, however, in the *physical arts* of music and dance as compared with the relatively *nonphysical arts* of art, theater, and literature. Because execution of the physical arts rests substantially on the artist's ability to use his or her lips, limbs, fingers, vocal chords, and other parts of the body, these parts must be kept in tone, much as athletes do in preparation for their activities. Anyone seeking an amateur career here, if it is to be truly fulfilling, must plan on training or practicing nearly every day. My studies of musicians suggest that any physical artist keen to improve at his or her art needs a minimum of forty-five to sixty minutes per session at one session per day at five days a week. The basic problem faced by these artists, both amateur and professional, is that they usually notice how their physical skills have atrophied after no more than two days away from their routine. French pianist and composer Robert Casadesus once remarked in an interview that he could tell from his playing when he took a day off and his wife could tell when he was away for two. Perceived decline of this sort is especially painful for the performer. This person must now try to recover lost technique and stamina, while suffering through some sessions of artistically inferior playing or dancing.

People seeking an amateur career in the nonphysical arts face a different routine. Their creativity flows more or less directly from the mind; it is not mediated significantly by a specialized physical capacity through which to express it. The readiness of the mind to respond with artistic ideas atrophies more slowly than the readiness of the body to implement them. Thus writers, actors, and painters, for example, need not train or practice with the regularity of musicians and dancers. Nevertheless, nonphysical artists are quick to point out that too much time away from the art leads to noticeable mental sluggishness, to slowness and fuzziness in expressing artistic ideas. In this respect, although it is unnecessary to pursue the art almost daily, these artists cannot spend, say, two weeks away from it without feeling the effects of this lapse.

So routine in the two types of fine art is important in its special way. People unfamiliar with the serious leisure activities requiring routine involvement often ask why anyone would want to bother with routines during their free time. "It sounds too much like work," they typically opine. Yet these amateurs would have it no other way, for it is through routine pursuit, however done, that they realize the uncommon, powerful rewards that come from executing well a complex activity. Playing around at the activity, as dabblers do, is unfulfilling for the amateur (and the professional). More on this in chapter 6.

Training

Although in days gone by some amateur participants in some of the fine arts were self-taught, a modest level of formal training is now the norm in all of them. To reach the kind of competence needed to perform these arts at the least demanding adult level, most neophytes in music should expect to spend a minimum of a year in private lessons. Those in art, dance, and theater should expect to complete an established program of classes. This estimate presumes for the physical artists close to one-hour stints of individual practice between lessons or classes. Would-be poets and novelists can get formal training in writing courses, which are also organized into programs. Here, too, homework is required to improve literary skills. Formal training in the entertainment arts is usually unavailable, although in principle it is as necessary as in the fine arts. Consider magic, stand-up comedy, and the other variety arts, in which amateurs commonly develop their skills by reading manuals, watching professionals and other amateurs, arranging sessions of tutelage with professionals, and learning through trial-and-error. By contrast, if you are interested in public speaking programs, search online for your city using these or similar keywords.

In general, executing the fine and entertainment arts appeals to all ages; only rarely does their execution interest only one or a few age categories, although physical conditions such as arthritis, heart disease, and stiffening joints can force older amateurs and professionals out of the physical arts. They may also prevent would-be older amateurs from entering them. To the extent that mental acuity declines with age, similar impediments may crop up in the nonphysical arts as well. But age is not otherwise a barrier to participation in these endeavors. Indeed, some of the adverse mental and physical effects of aging can be mitigated somewhat by pursuing a vigorous amateur career in an art. That being said, it is a good idea in any art to take it up no later than middle adulthood, if possible. All neophytes need time to develop the competence required to perform their pursuit at a fulfilling level.

Social World

Each art form has its own social world, itself a main attraction for many amateurs. To participate in this world is to be in the swim. The amateur in the collective arts of dance, music, and theater is anchored in the artistic ensemble to which this person belongs: the band, chorus, sketch team, dance company, theater group, or puppet troupe. In the collective arts amateurs of varying levels of commitment and competence mix to present public performances, where they are sometimes joined by the occasional professional. Some participants augment their amateur involvement by becoming volunteer helpers with the administrative duties that seem to proliferate in many artistic organizations.

Around this core lie peripheral services provided by suppliers (of strings, costumes, music), repair people (for musical instruments), stagehands, make-up artists, lighting specialists, and many others. Add to all this the diverse venues where the art is performed, as in theaters, nightclubs, dance floors, concert halls, and so on. Furthermore, some amateurs receive periodicals bearing on their art, possibly as part of their membership in a society or association established to promote it. Live, televised, and recorded performances by professionals and other amateurs make up still another part of the complex social worlds of many of the collectively involved artists.

The social worlds of the individual arts differ substantially from those of the collective arts. The individual arts include art and literature as well as the performing arts of magic, variety, pantomime, tap dancing, stand-up comedy, and piano and accordion playing. It is true that writers, painters, and magicians sometimes establish local clubs for the purpose of presenting their art and discussing common needs and problems. But, depending on the art, they commonly work at it alone at home, onstage, in a studio, or at another appropriate location. The social worlds of the individual artists are organized around such places as well as around various opportunities to present their works publicly in bookstores, galleries, theaters, festivals, auditoriums, and exhibitions. Reviews of these works constitute another part of their world, but only to the extent that critics pay attention to amateur productions. Such intermediaries as editors, publishers, foundries (for some sculptors), and piano tuners also play an extremely important role in the leisure lives of many of these serious amateurs.

SPORT

By sport I mean inter-human, competitive, physical activity based on a recognized set of rules.[3] These defining criteria are important, for as will become evident in the next chapter the label of sport is sometimes applied to activities that fail to meet them.

In the eyes of the spectators sport is patently an entertainment. And whereas many players recognize that spectators see sport in these terms, the former define it quite differently. They see it first and foremost as a game controlled by rules, where the main goals are to win and find fulfillment in playing that game. In the eyes of the amateurs and professionals who play them, the following sports and games amount to much more than mere diversion. For them these activities are either devotee work or serious leisure. The parenthetic designations in this list indicate that the amateurs have counterparts for whom the sport is a livelihood. The sports marked with an asterisk are those played at both the professional and the elite amateur levels (defined below); descriptions of these sports are available in encyclopedias and online.

Team Sports (professional)

- football
- basketball*
- baseball
- hockey*
- soccer*
- rugby
- cricket
- roller hockey

Team Sports (elite amateur)

- field hockey
- yachting
- bobsledding
- volleyball
- rowing
- water polo
- synchronized swimming

Individual Sports (professional)

- boxing*
- tennis (including doubles)
- golf
- squash
- racquetball (including doubles)
- jai alai (including doubles)
- equestrian events*
- bowling
- figure skating*
- auto racing

- motorcycle racing
- rodeo (calf roping, steer wrestling, bull riding, etc.)

Individual Sports (elite amateur)

- handball
- swimming
- diving
- track and field events
- archery
- badminton (including doubles)
- martial arts
- speed skating
- alpine skiing and snowboarding
- cross-country skiing
- ski jumping
- cycling
- shooting (firearms)
- weight lifting
- gymnastics
- wrestling[4]
- fencing
- canoe and kayak racing
- luge
- sailing

What about government-supported elite amateurs competing in the Olympic Games and other international contests? Are they not basically professional? True, some countries still officially deny this de facto status, even while joining with various commercial sponsors to provide these athletes with room and board and even money for casual spending. Such support enables the athletes to devote themselves full-time to perfecting their sport, much as real professional players do. Why these arrangements? Because excellence in elite and professional sport is often a source of national identity and pride. Nevertheless, though professional both by definition and by level of competence, elite amateurs usually lack the glamor and respect enjoyed by the pros. These amateurs are highly influential in their own social worlds, however. Here they are powerful role models for the much larger number of ordinary participants.

Training

Sport is by definition a physical undertaking. So here a routine practice and training schedule is as necessary as in the physical arts and is justified with the same reasons. Moreover, the minimally effective period of daily training appears to be approximately the same: around forty-five to sixty minutes. Finally, as in the arts, playing any sport as a dabbler brings comparatively little satisfaction once the player becomes familiar with the rewards attainable from playing as a dedicated amateur (or professional).

Training in the amateur-professional, amateur-elite sports is always formal in one way or another. Initially, the neophyte joins a basketball or football team, for example, and receives training from a coach. Novices in most of the individual sports typically start by taking lessons from a professional or elite amateur. This is not true, however, for wrestling and track and field. Here athletes join a "team" of individual contestants, getting their instruction and criticism from its coach. Some golf and tennis amateurs start their sports careers on similar teams. Rodeo and auto and motorcycle racing are the only sports in this list in which novices learn informally, accomplished in the main by watching, asking questions, and sometimes arranging regular tutelage.

The physical nature of sport sets age limits with the same relentlessness as the physical arts do. But it is also true that sports vary widely in the physical intensity and bodily flexibility needed to play them at a fulfilling amateur level. Age forty is more or less the upper limit for the contact sports of football, rugby, hockey, boxing, rodeo, and wrestling. And few people seem to compete beyond this age in the highly aerobic sports of hockey, rowing, soccer, basketball, figure skating, field hockey, and speed skating. In other highly aerobic sports—cycling, racquetball, swimming, and cross-country skiing—age-graded competitions are common, an arrangement that extends the age limits considerably.

Moreover, people in their sixties (and some even their seventies) swim, cycle, and cross-country ski for exercise and conditioning without competing. That is, they don't treat these activities as sports. The same may be said for tennis when not played in tournaments and similar competitions. Finally, people in their seventies participate extensively in the sports of low physical intensity, such as golf, shooting, bowling, yachting, and sailing. People of many ages also find great satisfaction in baseball and cricket.

In general, the amateur sports career advances through the same set of stages as its physical counterpart in art and entertainment. Nevertheless, the two careers do diverge in several specific ways. Thus, for many amateurs in sport the transition to the establishment stage is often abrupt and clear. That is, they are invited to join an adult team (e.g., park board, university, industrial) or a local club or they are placed on a list of qualified competitors. Furthermore, among all the artists, only those in the more rigorous forms of dance are familiar with the unyielding age limits to high-aerobic or high-impact activity felt in many of the sports.

Social World

Each of the sports listed here has its own social world. In amateur team sport, the team itself and its coach occupy the center of the social world of its members. Games, usually held once a week, and practices, often held two or three times a week, make up another part of this core. Less central, but certainly enjoyable, are the post-practice and post-game get-togethers with teammates. Important peripheral services both in the team and the individual sports include judges, referees, trainers, and equipment sales and repair.

The social world of the amateur athlete in the individual sports revolves around a particular kind of competition site—for example, courts, tracks, swimming pools, and skating rinks and arenas. These athletes both practice and compete here, and here they meet likeminded enthusiasts. In Canada and Great Britain, among other countries, this core also includes the clubs that organize many of these sports and any coaches who work there for either no remuneration or a small fee. In the United States the individual sports are mostly organized by high schools, colleges, and universities.

The core of the social world of team sport also takes in the league in which the participant's team plays, the other teams in the league, the schedule of games, and the ever-changing team standings of wins and losses. The equivalent core in the individual sports consists of the usual series of competitions (meets, races, matches) entered throughout the season. Though standings are often not calculated here, individual rankings certainly are. When clubs compete in these events through representation by their individual members, winning or losing against the other competing clubs is reckoned according to the accumulated successes and failures of the individuals.

The professionals and elite amateurs make up still another important part of the core of the social world of amateur sport. These stars are deeply honored as exemplars of excellence in the sport in question. Moreover, they may be hired to coach a team or a club or, more rarely, an individual athlete. Some are invited to give clinics or demonstrations. During informal encounters with the professionals and elite amateurs, ordinary amateurs learn about life in the "big time." Here, to help them perform better, these lucky amateurs may also pick up some invaluable tips on technique, equipment, strategy, and other pertinent concerns. Sometimes the stars communicate through nationally or internationally distributed magazines like *Bicycling*, *Golf Digest*, and *Cross-Country Skier* or through the newsletter of a national or international organization.

SCIENCE

My research on serious leisure involvements in science revealed three kinds of participants: observers, armchair participants, and applied scientists. The observers are amateurs; they directly experience their objects of interest through scientific inquiry. The armchair participants are liberal arts hobbyists who pursue their interests largely, if not wholly, through reading (more on them in the next chapter). They hold to their approach either because they prefer it to observation or because they lack the time, equipment, opportunity, or physical stamina to go into the field or laboratory. The applied scientists, who are also amateurs, express their knowledge of a branch of science in some practical way. As far as we know, the most active group of applied amateurs is found in computer science.

Amateur observers vary much more than their professional counterparts in their level of knowledge and degree of willingness and ability to contribute original data to their science. Thus the observers pursue their scientific activity as one of three subtypes: apprentice, journeyman, or master.[5] Further, some of them find that their leisure career in their science has them advancing from apprentice to journeyman and possibly on to master.[6] Such passage is an inexact process, however, for the acquisition of knowledge, experience, and personal confidence is always gradual and at times hesitant.

Scientific apprentices are learners. They hope to absorb enough about their discipline, its research procedures, and its instrumentation to function as journeymen and eventually, perhaps, as masters. As their knowledge about their science grows, some apprentices select a specialty, becoming learners here as well. Scientific apprentices, unlike their opposite number in the trades, are normally independent; formal association with a master over a prescribed period of time is unheard of. Even at this stage, these practitioners have the freedom to explore their science on their own, which they do mostly by reading and listening to talks. At this point, however, they are typically incapable of making an original contribution to it.

Journeymen are knowledgeable, reliable practitioners who can work independently in one or a few specialties. They have advanced far enough to make original contributions to their science. Yet it is a matter of personal definition as to whether an amateur has reached this level of expertise. The amateurs I interviewed were typically modest, even humble, about their attainments. They seemed to sense when they were effectively apprentices, when they had much to learn, and when they needed supervision in, say, excavating an archaeological site or more experience in working up a valid set of observations. Even journeymen may feel "inadequate" after comparing themselves with the local professionals with whom a number of them have frequent contact. Journeymen are always learning, expanding their grasp of the discipline as a whole, and continually absorbing new developments pertaining to their specialties. The same holds for the masters as well as for the professionals.

The masters actually contribute to their science, most often by collecting original data on their own that help advance the field. They are aware of certain knowledge gaps in their specialties, and they know how to make the observations that could conceivably close or at least narrow those gaps. To this end, they systematically collect the relevant data and publicize them through talks, reports, and journal articles. Any amateur can contribute through serendipity, such as by fortuitously discovering a new celestial object. But masters systematically seek new data through programs they design (e.g., digging their own archaeological sites) or coordinate with others (e.g., working as part of a team spread across the country to observe a lunar occultation).[7]

Master amateur research projects are chiefly exploratory and descriptive, however, with the theorizing and hypotheses-testing being left to the pros. Nevertheless, when these projects are properly carried out, validation of the researcher's status as a master follows. Amateurs and professionals alike acknowledge the individual's contributions, journal articles are accepted for publication, and the occasional local speaking invitation may be received.

In principle every science can have an amateur wing, for no science formally restricts data collection within its domain. Yet, as the following list demonstrates, only some sciences actually have established amateur components. It is probable that the others effectively, although inadvertently, discourage amateur participation. This they do by being highly abstract or by requiring equipment or training largely inaccessible to nonprofessionals. The following sciences have active amateur wings and, in harmony with the preceding discussion, are primarily exploratory and descriptive. Moreover, each has local variations in its objects of study so extensive that its professional core needs help to cover them all. Here, the amateurs in the area are keen to lend a hand.

Physical Sciences

- physics
- computer science
- astronomy
- mineralogy
- meteorology

Biological Sciences

- ornithology
- entomology
- botany

Social Sciences

- history
- archaeology

Reading in a science and collecting descriptive data on one of its relevant research problems are two core activities in these amateur pursuits. Amateurs in physics are concentrated in the branch of upper atmosphere or space physics where they explore the radio waves as ham radio operators. Amateurs in computer science explore the applications of the latest hardware and software available for personal computers. Amateurs in astronomy describe meteor showers, stellar and lunar occultations, variable star activity, and other celestial phenomena. Those in mineralogy study the nature and distribution of rocks and minerals in a particular geographic area, usually the one where they live.

Amateurs in meteorology participate in local weather forecasting. In ornithology they systematically observe the behavior and habitats of birds. Amateur entomologists do much the same, focusing on insects instead. Amateur botanists collect, identify, and preserve specimens of various kinds of plant life found in a given geographic area.

Amateur historians nearly always write in the branch of their discipline known as local history, typically concentrating on their own town or region. It is the same for amateur archaeologists, who search for prehistoric relics and sites of human use and habitation, describing and preserving what they find. In most of the fields listed here, the amateurs follow the lead of their professional counterparts and specialize, as in the study of song birds, binary stars, or mushrooms (mycology).

The background knowledge needed for a career in amateur science comes from a variety of sources, most of which require the participant to read published material. Credit and noncredit courses, which combine reading and lectures, are often available in the aforementioned sciences at colleges and universities throughout the West. In addition, articles bearing on different specialities are published from time to time in periodicals intended for the amateur market of these disciplines. Finally, the amateurs, possibly in collaboration with one or more of the local professionals, may establish a local club. Here they meet as often as weekly for workshops, reports on research by their colleagues, and the occasional lecture delivered by a professional.

Even though apprentices hardly gain their knowledge over night, they seem to progress more quickly to the stage of journeyman than the other types of amateurs mentioned in this chapter progress to an equivalent stage in their fields. For the latter, compared with acquiring intellectual knowledge, more time is needed to polish skills and harness them according to the appropriate principles of implementation. As a reasonable estimate, it takes approximately six months for the typical amateur scientist to develop into a scientific journeyman.

Social World

The local club, which may be a chapter of a national organization, forms part of the core of the amateur scientist's social world. This core is further made up of the places where research is conducted (e.g., excavation sites in archaeology, forests in ornithology, archives and libraries in local history). And since amateur science is intellectual work, a home study of some sort is indispensable and therefore another core feature of this social world. The master amateurs and the professionals of the science inhabit the center of this world. Within this nucleus the amateurs collect data for the pros, who use it either to generate new propositions about the object of study or to test existing hypotheses bearing on it. The social world of amateur science also has a number of important peripheral members, notably equipment vendors and journal editors.

What makes all the amateur social worlds truly distinct is that professionals play a central role in them. In most instances they are locally available so the amateurs may rub elbows with them, pattern their scientific lives after them, and marvel at their feats made possible by full-time devotion to the activity. Although not all professionals are good role models or blessed with agreeable personalities, a sufficient number of them come close enough to these ideals to win a place of honor in one of the worlds of avocational science. They may only rarely be seen in person, but their influence is both wide and deep, in part because of their frequent appearance in the discipline's print and electronic media.

It is the absence of this professional counterpart that most clearly distinguishes hobbyists from amateurs. Nevertheless, looking solely at the former, this lack should never be misunderstood as a mark of inferiority, simplicity, or triviality. As will become evident in the next chapter, no serious leisure hobby can be described in such terms.

GETTING STARTED AS AN AMATEUR

When people enter any of the amateur, hobbyist, or volunteer activities discussed in this book, they do so by way of one or more of the doors to its social world. This is well illustrated in the fine arts and entertainment fields considered next. In the main, a person gets started here by taking lessons or courses on how to perform the art, observing amateur and professional expressions of it, talking with its experienced practitioners (amateur or professional), and, above all, actually executing it. In some of the arts, beginners also learn by reading instructional material. It bears repeating that, to learn any one of these arts, the beginner must observe (look, listen) repeatedly a great many exemplars of the art. In this manner the beginner internalizes the principles commonly used to discern good work and, with these standards in mind, can start setting goals for his or her own serious leisure career in that field.

Music

Private lessons, or a bit more rarely class instruction, in voice or on an instrument constitute the main port of entry into the world of music. None of the five forms—jazz, choral singing, operatic singing, chamber music, and orchestral music—can be executed at a reasonably fulfilling level without a certain amount of formal training of this nature. Private lessons are usually available for voice and the more popular instruments (guitar, flute, cello, trumpet, trombone, violin, piano, clarinet, percussion, saxophone, and accordion) in all but the smallest and most remote North American communities. To locate a teacher, look in the yellow pages or online at Yellowpages.com (or YP.com) under such headings as "Music Colleges" and "Music Teachers." But since not all music teachers are listed here, ask a musical friend or acquaintance to suggest someone. Established amateurs and professionals typically know a great number of vocalists and instrumentalists and can, using these informal connections, put the novice in touch with an effective teacher. Other good sources of information include high school music teachers, college and university departments of music, and the musicians in the community's amateur and professional musical groups. The personnel working at the music stores can usually suggest teachers for the instruments they sell and rent. Some even give lessons themselves. Employees at the office of the local union of the American Federation of Musicians of the United States and Canada know of many of the music teachers in town. People interested in a jazz or folk music instrument might seek information on teachers from the local jazz or folk-music club. However the teacher is found, the beginner should indicate the type of music he or she eventually wants to play (i.e., jazz, folk, rock, country, orchestral), for once they have imparted the basics of the instrument, teachers tend to specialize in one of these types.

Class instruction is available on some instruments, most commonly as part of a continuing education program in which students learn mostly by playing in a small band, chamber group, or symphony orchestra. And choral training is by nature collective, consisting of group instruction or personal instruction offered through the chorus or choir. Although continuing education courses are sometimes available here, too, most adult amateurs seem to enter choral singing through a church choir, community chorus, or barbershop chorus. College and university students may have access to a chorus or an orchestra at their institution, although these groups usually accept experienced singers only.

Beginning instrumentalists buy, rent, or borrow the musical instrument on which they intend to become proficient. It is wise to seek advice on this matter from an experienced musician, often one's music teacher. Except for those playing the pipe organ or the orchestral percussion instruments, established amateurs almost always own their instruments. But beginners will want to determine their commitment to this kind of serious leisure before making such a purchase, which is likely to be costly.

Dance

Although private lessons are available in ballroom and country and western dancing, beginners in these and the other forms of dance (jazz, tap, line, ballet, choral, modern) most commonly get their start in classes. The yellow pages and the Internet offer possibly the best lists of the community's instructional opportunities in this art under such headings as "Dance Clubs," "Dance Studios," and "Dance Academies." Insider advice on which studio to select may be sought from friends and acquaintances who know the local scene for the dance in question or, for jazz, ballet, and modern dance, from the dance department of a nearby college or university. In fact, such departments have their own introductory courses in jazz, ballet, and modern dance, which are usually open to all full- and part-time students attending the college or university. Performing dance troupes, both amateur and professional, also have information on how to enter their kind of dance.

Theater

One or two semester-length drama courses are normally all that are needed to learn the basic principles of acting. The same can be said for puppetry. The courses are noncredit when taught in a continuing education program, whereas they must be taken for credit when taught at a college or university. In the latter, however, students are often allowed to enroll in the introductory courses even though they are majoring in fields other than drama. Stores selling and renting theatrical costumes, supplies, and equipment (they are listed in the yellow pages) may be able to steer beginners toward the classes they need. In the final analysis, however, most of the art of drama is learned onstage, by landing a part in a play and then working with the director to interpret it appropriately and imaginatively. As for beginning courses in cinematic production, they are comparatively rare. But such courses do turn up occasionally in the nondegree programs in continuing education and regularly in the degree programs in cinematic production offered by a number of community colleges and technical schools.

Beginners in the entertainment dramatic arts other than sketch, puppetry, cinematic production, and commercial community theater acquire their fundamentals in a strikingly different way. This is necessary because formal courses of the kind described for the preceding arts are simply unavailable in most communities. Thus these beginners must get their start by observing the performances of competent amateurs and professionals and by talking with them about how they learn their art, organize their routines into shows of twenty to forty minutes, and book opportunities to present the shows in public. Budding magicians can also receive advice on these questions from established magicians working at the local magician supply stores and from members of one of the local magic clubs (ask at the supply stores about these). New participants in comedy hang around the comedy clubs in their community, watching the art in its many expressions, talking with performers, and, eventually, presenting their own five-minute "spots" on amateur night. In both magic and comedy there is usually a local professional or two who offer individual or group lessons. Inquire at the comedy clubs and magic clubs and supply stores about this kind of instruction.[8]

Clowning and juggling are learned much the same way. The local professionals and some of the local amateurs can be contacted directly through their own enterprise or indirectly through an agent (see "Entertainment and Entertainment Bureaus" in the yellow pages and on the Internet). The personnel at the magic supply stores may know a clown or juggler who gives lessons or at least is willing to talk informally about how to learn their art. Finally, in those North American cities where the American Guild of Variety Artists has a local union, office staff may keep a list of such people.

Art

Beginning amateurs in art can learn the rudiments of painting, drawing, sculpting, printmaking, and photography through the appropriate noncredit courses given in continuing education or the appropriate credit courses given by the art schools and the college and university art departments. Alternatively, they may enroll in the beginners' classes offered at some of the local art studios and art supplies stores. To locate these, consult the yellow pages in the telephone directories of the larger cities, looking under such headings as "Art Lessons" and "Art Instruction." Art suppliers not themselves in the instruction business can normally be counted on to furnish a decent overview of the local opportunities in art instruction for beginners.

Commercial instruction in photography—instruction offered by a business establishment—can be obtained at some studios of local professional photographers (look under headings such as "Schools—Photography" in the yellow pages). Apart from basic instruction in drawing, no formal training exists for would-be cartoonists and caricaturists. Instruction in printing should be sought through the noncredit courses offered in continuing education or through the credit courses given in an established graphic design program at a technical school. Instructional manuals in all areas of art are available from the supplies outlets. But be aware that evaluation by an experienced artist of the beginner's painting or photography, for example, is absolutely essential if the latter is to find fulfillment in the activity and enjoy a leisure career there. The instructor usually meets this need for students enrolled in his or her course. Again, it should be understood that manuals serve most effectively as supplements to rather than substitutes for courses and lessons.

Literature

Aspiring writers should search the catalogs of the colleges, universities, and continuing education programs for introductory courses on writing fiction, nonfiction, and poetry. Some of the college and university courses may have prerequisites, commonly one or two literature courses, which invariably reduce their accessibility to a relatively small number of full- and part-time students. Although there are books for writers, these resources are never fully sufficient, for beginners especially need "editing," need to have their work criticized by seasoned authors. The teachers of the introductory courses fill this crucial role in the first instance.

Sport

Generally speaking, the sports are one of the easiest forms of serious leisure to enter, with most of the sports and the ways of entering them being well known. Indeed many adult amateurs in the collective sports began their athletic careers there as adolescents and, although they may have momentarily reduced their participation at some point in their adult years, they are hardly beginners when they reenter. To a lesser degree, the same can be said for the players of many of the individual sports. For anyone, then, getting started in a sport is problematic only if this person is a tyro.

But, in some team sports the teams are composed of disproportionate numbers of players who joined the team with no prior experience in the sport; these include yachting, rowing, bobsledding, water polo, and synchronized swimming. Few adults or high school students are likely to get the opportunity to participate in these sports, even if they live in communities where they are routinely played. A beginner living in a community where people yacht or bobsled, for example, faces two problems if he or she wants to become involved there: how to contact a team and how to wangle an invitation to join it. Perhaps the most effective way of solving these problems is to hang around the places where people engage in the activity: the wharf, river, bobsled run, swimming pool. Talk to the participants, asking about the nature of the activity, the ways a person can become involved, and the kinds of qualifications one is expected to have. In some communities these sports are organized in clubs, which makes access easier as long as they can be located. Check the yellow pages under such headings as "Clubs" and "Associations" or inquire at a nearby college or university in the unit variously known these days as the faculty (or department) of recreation, leisure studies, kinesiology, or physical education.

Adult beginners in some of the individual sports may get started by taking lessons. This is certainly a common approach for novices in golf, tennis, bowling, swimming, diving, archery, gymnastics, figure skating, and the equestrian events. Lessons in golf, tennis, bowling, swimming, diving, and gymnastics are sometimes advertised in the yellow pages. Alternatively, one can inquire at a golf or tennis club or a municipal swimming pool. Supplies and equipment stores specializing in these sports often maintain a list of instructors, which is where a beginner should seek such information for archery and figure skating. Instruction in any of these sports as well as in squash, handball, racquetball, badminton, ski jumping, and alpine and cross-country skiing may also be offered from time to time in small classes given in a continuing education program or in an equivalent community-oriented program sponsored by a college or university recreation or kinesiology department. Instruction in alpine skiing is frequently given on-site at the ski hills. Community sports centers, the Young Men's Christian Association (YMCA), and the Young Women's Christian Association (YWCA) also offer lessons and playing opportunities in a number of these sports. Classes in target shooting are sometimes available at the firing ranges in the area (see the yellow pages under a heading like "Rifle and Pistol Ranges"). Finally, the yellow pages classification of "Riding Academies" or its equivalent will help the reader find instruction in the equestrian events.

A few of the individual sports must be approached by a beginner much as he or she would approach the team sports of yachting, bobsledding, and the like: by hanging around the scene and showing an interest by asking questions. These sports include rodeo and auto and motorcycle racing. The remaining sports—luge, judo, boxing, cycling, jai alai, speed skating, canoe racing, weight lifting, track and field events—are highly specialized and often organized in clubs (or gyms for weight lifters). A combination of frequenting areas around the scene and inquiring at the club's office are two fruitful ways to explore entry into these sports. Equipment stores, particularly those in cycling and canoeing, are useful centers of information about races and the ways to participate in them. Wrestling can only be entered through a college or university team; this limits participation to registered students.

Science

The ubiquity of the amateur science clubs certainly facilitates entry into a number of the amateur sciences. But finding the club may prove to be a challenge, since few are listed in the telephone directory. One way around this obstacle is to contact the appropriate department at a college or university: the departments of geology or geography for mineralogy, department of physics for astronomy, departments of archaeology or anthropology for archaeology, department of history for local history, and department of computer science for amateur computer science. Note that in large universities the three biological sciences are often organized as either separate departments or quasi-autonomous subdivisions of a general department of biology.

In addition, the community's planetarium may know of the local astronomy club, even if it does not actually house it. And the local office of Environment Canada or the National Weather Service (USA) may have contact with the meteorology club in the area. Museums specializing in the history of the community and surrounding area may be extensively involved with the local history and archaeology societies. And natural history museums often have ties with the region's amateur entomology and ornithology clubs as well as with certain individual members of those clubs whose work enhances their collections. Although they seem to cater chiefly to hobbyists, the shops selling lapidary equipment and supplies may nevertheless maintain up-to-date information about the local mineralogy club.

The amateur science clubs are sometimes listed in the yellow pages under the rubric of "Clubs" or that of "Societies." Perusing these sections may be the only way to track down the local ham, or amateur, radio group as well as the ever growing number of computer clubs springing up everywhere in North America.

POSITIVE SIMPLICITY IN AMATEURISM

Some amateur activities are hugely expensive, others moderately so, and some are downright cheap. I am referring here to indispensable expenses—those that must be borne if the amateur is to participate at a fulfilling level.

The more costly arts include music, painting, photography, printmaking, sculpting, and art cinematic production. In these fields equipment and supplies (e.g., instruments, cameras, paints) or essential processes (e.g., bronzing, photographic printing) are often dear. In sport some fields are known for their expenses, among them golf, tennis, ice hockey, cycling, cross-country skiing, alpine skiing, yachting, sailing equestrian activities, and auto and motorcycle racing. Here the main cost is usually equipment (including horses), but maintenance, insurance, and club membership can also be major expenses, as in yachting, tennis, golf, equestrianism, and vehicle racing. Amateur science is normally not found in this league. Nevertheless, avocational astronomers, botanists, and entomologists might come close with the purchase of a state-of-the-art telescope or microscope.

At the other end of the cost spectrum lie the amateur activities that cost little or nothing to engage in. In the arts, apart from lessons, singing, acting, sketching with pencil or charcoal, line dancing, public speaking, and writing (assuming the writer has already bought a computer for general use) require negligible expenditure. This is the nonconsumptive leisure described in the introduction. Meanwhile, the rest of the amateur activities discussed in this chapter fall between the no-cost and high-cost poles, demanding of their enthusiasts usually manageable expenses to reach fulfillment. In this group the price of a membership in a gym, swimming facility, sport club, dance group, or music organization may well constitute the most substantial cost of the activity.

Retirees on the hunt for an amateur activity or two with which they can identify and for which they have some talent have a good range of them from which to choose. Although their financial situation will help guide their choices, that situation offers far more flexibility than most people realize. This is where positive simplicity enters the picture. It prompts people to ask questions like these: Should I buy a new car (the old one runs decently) or put my discretionary money toward some advanced golf lessons and a better set of clubs? Should I buy the high-quality violin I have always wanted, knowing how it will improve my musicianship? Should I, as an expert surfer, use my money for trips to some of the world's finest surfing areas?

Money needed to pursue or improve the pursuit of an amateur activity may also be found by cutting the costs of routine living. That is, positive simplicity—that intended to facilitate serious leisure—suggests that frugal amateurs can save cash by not hiring services they can do themselves. So, on the one hand, assuming as a retiree that you have the time as well as the skill and knowledge, you might paint your own house, service your own car, cook your meals at home and avoid restaurants, or launder and press your own clothes. The money saved would be used on what we discussed in chapter 1 as facilitative leisure consumption. On the other hand, if money is no object, you could hire these services and use the time gained to play a sport, take up ballroom dancing, do research on birds, and the like—to find fulfillment. A parallel option in this vein is to pursue a line of devotee work, find fulfillment in it, and hire such services as a way of freeing up time for more devotee activity. Of course, strictly speaking, this person is not or is no longer a retiree. Such people can have their retirement cake and eat it too.

The larger point in all this is to inspire you to take the initiative, be your own agent, and fashion a leisure lifestyle that maximizes your opportunities to develop yourself as an individual. The financial resources for such a goal are important, but a shortfall in this regard does not necessarily mean that the goal is lost. Positive simplicity can light the way, guiding the individual to amateur activities that are exciting, available, and affordable, although often with some adjustments in meeting life's nonwork obligations.

Chapter Four

Hobbies

> Do what you love. Know your own bone; gnaw at it, bury it, unearth it, and gnaw it still.
>
> Henry David Thoreau

Doing what you love should, you might think, be the theme of the preceding chapter on amateur activities. After all, amateurs are *amators*, the Latin word for "lover." Such linguistic subtleties aside, hobbyists love what they do just as much as the amateurs love their activities. And Thoreau is not so picky. For him, "what you love" may be an amateur activity, a hobbyist pastime, or even a volunteer role. His advice is to get to know it and then stick with it. Thoreau was, in effect, writing about the serious pursuits, for the "bone" in question could have been devotee work just as well as serious leisure.

The amateur activities described in the preceding chapter are the most restrictive of the three types of serious leisure. Executing them at a fulfilling level requires routine training and practice in art, sport, and entertainment, while science requires extensive acquisition of knowledge and, possibly, development of technique. This restrictiveness is one of the reasons why I estimate that no more than 20 percent of the North American population pursues an amateur career of some sort. Such rigor is by no means everyone's cup of tea.

HOBBIES: ACCESSIBLE LEISURE

My experience in serious leisure research suggests, however, that the proportion of hobbyists is significantly larger. This hunch stems from the observation that many hobbies are highly accessible. In spite of certain exceptions, most of them are learned informally, commonly by reading books or articles, listening to CDs or DVDs, and talking with other hobbyists. Acquiring knowledge in this manner is relatively inexpensive and easily molded around the enthusiast's work, leisure, and family schedules. Furthermore, many hobbies can be pursued within a personal timetable, having no scheduled meetings, practices, rehearsals, or public matches or performances. Hobbies learned fully or partly through adult education or online courses are at odds with these observations, in that there is both a fee to pay and a schedule to keep.

Furthermore, though it is often relatively inexpensive to launch a hobby, it may be costly to continue in it. Some items make expensive collectibles, some equipment used for constructing or repairing things is costly. Some hobbyist fly fishers, cross-country skiers, and animal breeders sink large sums of money into their pastimes, not unlike the amateurs who run up sizable family debts buying a good violin, telescope, or set of golf clubs. In this sense, then, certain hobbies may be no more accessible than many of the amateur activities.

There are two additional points to make about hobbies before proceeding with our discussion of the different types. First, when compared with the other durable benefits of a hobby, its monetary return is secondary. The studies of hobbyists support this proposition in that remuneration has never been mentioned as a reason for engaging in this kind of serious leisure. In other words, neither hobbies nor amateur pursuits are viewed primarily as supplements to the participant's main income; they are not "second jobs." In fact, a clear devotion emerges with reference to these forms of serious leisure, leading the hobbyist to pursue them despite possible or even actual financial loss. Indeed, even if this person did earn a substantial amount of money in the pursuit, this would be but one reward of many and, according to the evidence at hand, one of the least significant. Thus "sideline" businesses, including some so-called "hobby farms," because they constitute a partial livelihood, are logically excluded from consideration as true hobbies.

Second, some hobbyists fit more than one category, such as the builders of motorized model airplanes who ultimately fly their constructions in a nearby field. The classification of individual hobbyists also depends partly on the circumstances in which they undertake their activities. For example, swimmer number one, because he competes in swimming meets, will be discussed later as a player of a sport. Swimmer number two will be classified as an activity participant. She swims for the fulfillment she gets from developing and maintaining her skill, as well as for the exercise it provides.

The order of the hobbies covered in this chapter will be the same as that followed in chapter 2: collecting, making and tinkering, noncompetitive activity participation, hobbyist sports and games, and the liberal arts hobbies.

COLLECTING

The range and diversity of collectibles is enormous, as seen in stamps, paintings, rare books, violins, minerals, and butterflies. With experience, collectors become more knowledgeable about the social, commercial, and physical circumstances in which they acquire their cherished items. They also develop a sophisticated appreciation of these items, including a broad understanding of their historical and contemporary use, production, and significance.

Compared with commercial dealers, hobbyist collectors turn out to be a different breed. The dealers acquire their stock to make a living from its subsequent sales; their motives are clearly different from those driving the hobbyist collectors. Although the latter may try to make enough money selling a violin or painting to buy one of greater value, they are usually more interested in gaining a prestigious item for social and personal reasons, or possibly for hedging inflation, than in contributing directly to their livelihood. Additionally, unlike the typical dealer, many collectors hope to acquire an entire series or category of a collectible (e.g., all the posters of the Newport Jazz Festival, all the books in the Nancy Drew series).

The casual collecting of such things as matchbooks, beer bottles, and travel pennants is, at best, a marginal hobby. With such items there is nowhere near the equivalent complex of social, commercial, and physical circumstances to learn about; scant substantial aesthetic or technical appreciation to be cultivated; and no comparable level of understanding of production and use to be developed. Casual collecting is therefore most accurately classified as casual leisure, as simple diversion. As Allan Olmsted once put it, those who collect with little seriousness are "accumulators."[1]

Robert Overs developed a ninefold classification of collections.[2] I use his scheme here, though with several modifications and additions needed to bring it in line with the preceding definition of hobbyist activity.

Poster Collections

A poster is a large, printed picture designed for display in a public place. Some posters are issued as a series intended to publicize a regular or sporadic event. Examples include those created for recurrent arts festivals, academic conferences, and community fairs. Other posters announce one-shot events such as a photography exhibition, sports tournament, or program of courses. And still others convey an important message of some kind. Serious collectors specialize in certain kinds of posters, on which they gather information about their production and availability as well as about the event, message, or situation they are promoting.

Coin, Currency, and Medal Collections

With the exception of pin collecting, this is the field of numismatics. Overs classifies the coin and currency collections according to ancient, foreign, and domestic and the medals according to religious, military, commemorative, and novelty, a residual category. The hobbyist numismatist strives to learn about the social and political history of the items collected, as well as about their production and composition. The same may be said for the collectors of pins.

Stamp Collections

Philately is the name of this hobby. The serious philatelist not only collects stamps but also tries to acquire information about the social and economic circumstances underlying the decision to bring out each issue. Many stamps artistically express particular customs or values of a nation. They also greatly interest collectors.

Collections of Natural Objects

Among the chief natural challenges in nature collecting are learning what good specimens look like, where to find them, how to reach them efficiently, and how to acquire and preserve them. For example, an experienced collector of, say, grasshoppers, fossilized crustaceans, or conch shells will know to look on certain kinds of bushes, in certain types of rock, or along certain stretches of ocean beach, respectively. Hobbyist collectors also make an effort to learn what science has to say about their collectibles. Overs classifies these items as follows:

- fossils
- animal trophies and stuffed specimens
- moths, insects, and butterflies
- ferns and wild flowers
- leaves, pine cones, and other arboreal objects
- rocks, stones, and minerals
- pearls, seashells, starfish, sponges, and other oceanic objects

Each natural object lends itself to detailed study about its formation, natural history, and ambient environment.

Note that these collectors are not gatherers. Gathering refers to acquiring a resource for subsequent use in making something.[3] Thus, some people gather driftwood for sculpturing or home decoration. Others gather beach pebbles, sea shells, or beach glass (glass washed up on shore), which, for example, they assemble as mosaics or bottled decorations or for display as individual pieces. Gatherers are hobbyists of the maker and tinkering variety, not collectors (or casual leisure accumulators).

Model Collections

With so many different kinds of models to consider, collectors in this field have little choice but to specialize. Some collect models of trains, cars, ships, airplanes, or animals. Others go in for toys, kites, or weapons. Even then, some types of models are so diverse that those who collect them are forced by the limits imposed by time and money to concentrate on one or a few subcategories.

Doll Collections

Dolls reflect a great deal about the prevailing culture and practices at a particular time in a particular society. Perhaps this explains why collecting dolls appeals to both sexes.[4] Overs says that collectors are more interested in antique and speciality dolls than in modern toy dolls, which they consider the less aesthetically appealing of the two types.

Collections of Art Objects

Any type of object created with substantial artistry or craftsmanship—for instance, paintings, sculptures, and musical instruments—may be seen as worthy of serious collection. Some collectors in this area specialize in a particular kind of china or glassware (e.g., plates, figurines), while others center their attention on recordings or folk-art objects. Although some of these objects are mass produced, they are nevertheless beautiful and therefore regarded as worthy acquisitions.

Antique Collections

What is defined as "antique" and hence as collectible varies widely. As a general rule, furniture, equipment, decorations, and other items are considered antique if they were in use several generations ago and now seem quaint and outdated. Their strangeness makes them interesting in modern times, encouraging the collector to learn about their customary use and construction when they were in vogue. Among the most frequently collected antiques are toys, glass, cars, clocks, dishes, bottles, weapons, watches, furniture, photographs, and books and documents.

Contemporary Popular Culture Collections

Contrary to what was said at the beginning of this section, certain kinds of artifacts in modern popular culture *are* sufficiently profound to merit being labeled "collectible." These include collecting pins, comics, sports cards, and baseball caps. The collectors of pins search for the thousands of different manufactured emblems and ornamentations that people wear to publicize certain events, attitudes, and organizations. According to About.com, collectors tend to specialize in pins commemorating the Olympic Games, Disney productions, and the horses, people, and events of the equestrian world (see About.com under "pin collecting"). Olympic pin trading, in particular, has been in vogue in North America since the early 1980s. Moreover, since pins, comics, sports cards, and baseball caps may be treated as investments, the purely leisure motive of engaging in the activity is diluted for some collectors (sometimes substantially).

Careers in Collecting

Preparation time is short for the collector compared with, for example, that of the amateur. Having made the decision to collect, neophytes need only determine where to go and what to look for. Still, since some things are not worth collecting, they must study in advance the criteria used to identify collectible fossils, glass sculpture, or oil paintings. Collectors of natural objects will find that they need instruction on how to preserve what they find. Storage of collected items can also be plagued by problems, which the seasoned collector learns to solve. For instance, a dry environment can cause antique furniture to crack or book bindings to putrefy. Only accumulators collect with no preparation whatsoever.

Leisure careers in the collecting hobbies revolve heavily around acquisition, on acquiring objects and knowledge about them. As the collector gains more of both, this person's career advances, refracted from time to time in new directions by different contingencies and turning points encountered along the way. A contingency is an unintended event, process, or situation that occurs by chance, lying beyond the control of the person in the career. Stumbling onto a valuable antique in grandmother's attic is a contingency. A turning point is a juncture—a critical event or decision—at which the nature of the career changes significantly. For example, an avid poster collector is forced to cut back on purchases in her hobby because the price of posters has risen dramatically. Of note in this book is the fact that very few careers in collecting are limited to a particular age category.

The Collector's Social World

In many of the collecting hobbies, the corresponding social worlds are anchored in a local club or national organization and sometimes both. Although collecting itself is an individual activity, the clubs provide members with a place for showing kindred enthusiasts the items they have collected and garnering insider information on how to acquire the best specimens of their kind of collectible. Some collectors are aided in their search by dealers (e.g., in art, stamps, coins), who make up another part of the core of this social world. Meanwhile, the clubs take on a special importance for many of the dealers, who use them as outlets for displaying their wares and advertising their services.

The social worlds of some collectors are further made up of the people and establishments they must deal with to obtain the items they are searching for. Apart from patronizing the dealers, who are usually expensive, stamp collectors often develop sets of contacts—friends, acquaintances, relatives—who bring them stamps from time to time. On seeing a pin they like, collectors in this field approach its wearer in hope of trading another pin for the one desired. Antique collectors eventually hear about the shops most likely to carry items of interest to them, after which they set about perfecting the art of haggling with the staff in hope of buying at the best price. They and some other kinds of collectors also get into the habit of haunting auctions, garage sales, and flea markets. Some collectible items such as guns and stamps are presented periodically at shows. It is also true, however, that many collections are not at all social as just described. To pursue these hobbies, these collectors need only head for the woods or the shore or curl up on the couch with a good mail-order or online catalog.

MAKING AND TINKERING

Grouped under this heading are such enthusiasts as inventors, seamstresses, automobile repairers, and toy and furniture makers. Excluded from it are the do-it-yourself drudges who, to avoid the expense of a full-time tradesperson, for instance, paint the exterior of their houses. Their motives contrast sharply with those of the hobbyist home remodeler. Additionally, because they are both work roles and business roles, the occupations of commercial automobile repair, clothing manufacture, and pottery making are also excluded from consideration in this book.

Although it may seem odd, it is entirely consistent with the extended meaning of the "maker" part of this category to include within it those hobbyists who breed or display fish, birds, reptiles, and animals. This same heading also embraces the people who avocationally breed or display such animals as dogs, cats, sheep, horses, ferrets, and, in recent years in the mountainous areas of western North America, llamas. We return to these raisers and breeders later in this section.

Robert Overs's classification of "craft activities" provides the framework for the following discussion of the making and tinkering hobbies.

Cooking, Baking, and Candy Making

This category covers a wide variety of activities ranging from making candy and sausages to baking cakes, pies, cookies, and various kinds of breads. Some people find a substantial hobby in cooking ethnic specialities from traditional recipes. Others go in for decorating cakes or producing wine or beer. What is more, hobbyists in this area often use parties and holidays as special occasions for presenting the fruits of their labors.

Beverage Crafts

This is the classificatory home of those who make a hobby of producing their own wine, beer, liqueurs, and similar kinds of drink. Although books exist on these subjects, kits with instructions are also widely available in specialty stores, where one may also buy the necessary equipment and ingredients. Store personnel are usually good sources of advice on making the beverage they represent.

Decorating Activities

Overs lists two kinds of activities here, both of which are pursued with sufficient regularity to qualify as hobbies: arranging flowers and decorating small objects. The first is carried out using either fresh or artificial blooms, the latter having by far the greater durability. With some imagination and perseverance, a person can decorate any small object in an aesthetically pleasing way. Overs mentions etching pieces of glass and burning designs in wood. Hobbies have also developed around the embellishment of thimbles, washers, toothpicks, and drinking glasses, to name but a few possibilities. Decoupage (the art of decorating surfaces with cutouts) and collage (the art of making compositions from ordinary materials such as cloth, paper, and metal) further exemplify the decorating activities. Creating mobiles and stencils are two additional decorating activities.

Interlacing, Interlocking, and Knot-Making Activities

These activities include wickerwork and basket weaving as well as macramé and the other knot-making crafts. Fly-tying is a rather exclusive example of the latter. Quilting, knitting, weaving, and crocheting also fall under this heading, as do the hobbies of making hooked, braided, and woven rugs. Last but certainly not least are the crafts of lacework, embroidery, and tapestry.

Toy, Model, and Kit Assembly

This category spans an enormous variety of activities, running from making puppets (figures formed with a costumed hand), marionettes (figures manipulated by strings or wires), and dolls and doll furniture to constructing models of trains, cars, boats, airplanes, rockets, and the like. Some of these hobbyists spend their leisure building model houses or furniture, while others devote themselves to electronic projects made from kits (e.g., stereo tuner, craft store projects). Finally, repairing toys, models, and game and sports equipment may become a hobby for enthusiasts with a reasonably regular supply of projects from, say, their own children or grandchildren or the children in the neighborhood.

Paper Crafts

Hobbies in this category appealing to adults include scrapbook projects and papier-mâché constructions (technically a hybrid of sculpture and paper-cutting). Origami, the Oriental art of paper folding, employs a range of skills, some of which are highly evolved. Bookbinding is a supplementary craft used by hobbyists pursuing scrapbook projects and people wanting to bind their personal diaries.

Leather and Textile Crafts

Felt, cloth, and leather are the principal materials employed in these crafts. The supplementary craft of dyeing serves to embellish items made from these three. Hobbyists in this field turn out a great assortment of products using felt, cloth, or leather, either alone or in combination. Their most common fabrications include belts, gloves, purses, costumes, moccasins, and other articles of clothing. All this is accomplished through another hobby— namely, sewing.

Wood- and Metalworking Activities

One of the best known activities in this category is woodworking, the craft of utilizing hand and power tools to build everything from bookends and birdhouses to furniture and garden sheds. Equally rewarding are the metal projects, which draw on the hobbyist's welding and soldering skills, among others. Less common these days but nonetheless highly satisfying is the woodworking hobby of whittling. It is basically wood sculpture employing a knife instead of the chisels, gouges, and similar tools of conventional woodworking. Whittlers produce bowls, bookends, figurines, napkin rings, and a multitude of other objects.

Do-It-Yourself Activities

Earlier I mentioned the do-it-yourself drudge. Still, some people find some do-it-yourself projects to be quite agreeable, to be project-based leisure as described in chapter 2. Scattered single do-it-yourself projects do not, however, amount to a hobby. But keeping in good running order one's own home, and perhaps the homes of friends, relatives, and neighbors, can turn into a regular and most worthwhile pursuit. Such a pursuit requires an immense range of skills and knowledge applied to appliance repair, plumbing work, electrical work, and interior and exterior house construction and decoration. The last of these requires proficiency with tile, paint, varnish, siding, panels, roofing, drywall, and wallpaper, to mention some of the more common materials. Auto and small engine repair is also part of this list, again with the proviso that it be done regularly and primarily for leisure fulfillment. That hobbyists here occasionally save themselves money by avoiding commercial services in no way compromises their more fundamental serious leisure motive of seeking deeply rewarding activity for its own sake.

Raising and Breeding

Hobbyists who raise fish, birds, reptiles, and animals (usually cats, dogs, and horses) are makers of a special kind, in that they work with living organisms to perfect them according to certain standards. In addition to breeding a particular organism, these hobbyists may also find considerable reward in training or exhibiting what they have bred. The other main subcategory of raising and breeding is gardening, done either indoors or outdoors (or in both places). Depending on the location, this hobby may include raising plants, vines, shrubs, and trees. Some of these enthusiasts specialize in flowers, others in vegetables, and still others in nuts or fruits. Lawn care can be a hobby all on its own. Any of these pastimes may be done purely for display, competition, or personal fulfillment or a combination of the three.

Miscellaneous Crafts

Making candles and creating mosaics from such materials as glass, paper, and marble number among the hobbyist activities in this category. Furthermore, many adults and children find great fulfillment both in kite making and then in flying their constructions in a nearby field. Lapidary work—the art of cutting and polishing stones—is another miscellaneous craft. And then there are those who have passion for making interesting objects with beads, buttons, or plaster. Finally, the hobby of perfume making holds a unique allure for its enthusiasts.

Careers in Making and Tinkering

Many of the crafts depend for their deepest fulfillment on the development of substantial, specialized skills—for example, using a knife to whittle, a needle to sew, or a plane to make furniture. Other crafts, when pursued at their most rewarding levels, require considerable background knowledge. Cooking, do-it-yourself, and raising and breeding exemplify this prerequisite. Furthermore, hobbyists who assemble toys, models, and other objects from kits, like those who sew from patterns and cook from recipes, must have a talent for following often complicated instructions and paying strict attention to details. Those in the woodworking and metalworking fields along with some of the hobbyist do-it-yourselfers must also develop a capacity for creating their own plans and designs. Lastly, some of these activities can be most artistic, as is evident in working with rocks, making mosaics, and decorating different objects.

This is the stuff of the hobbyist career, which participants sense as they improve in skill, knowledge, artistry, attention to detail or a combination of these. In this sense careers in the making and tinkering hobbies resemble those in the amateur fields. But there are certain construction hobbies with comparatively light developmental requirements that revolve primarily around the accumulation of completed projects. These include some of the projects discussed under the headings of paper crafts, miscellaneous crafts, and interlacing and interlocking activities.

All these occasional, specialized requirements considered making and tinkering activities, on the whole, have always been a highly democratic road to serious leisure. They are open to the vast range of humankind across the world. Culturally learned preferences aside, none of these hobbies is limited to one sex, and all can appeal to the entire age range of adults possessing the physical and mental capacities to carry them out. It is quite possible that a properly conducted international survey would find more people seriously involved in making and tinkering than in any of the other four types of hobbies.

Social World

The social worlds associated with the different making and tinkering pastimes are equally varied, offering something for nearly everyone. Many of these activities allow participants to work alone, becoming socially tied up with others only to the extent necessary to get supplies for making their products and the extent needed to display them once completed. Hobbyists preferring greater social involvement can usually find a club to join. Or they may hang around the local shops that serve hobbyists with like interests, chatting with the clerks and customers. Some makers and tinkerers take advantage of the occasional noncredit course offered in their area. And in many of these hobbies, fairs and expositions (held annually, semiannually, sporadically) give them the opportunity to display their own work as well as view that of kindred enthusiasts. Furthermore, since many makers and tinkerers provide their products or services free of charge, often as gifts, they gain direct contact with a small number of outsiders. These outsiders are also part of the participants' social world.

ACTIVITY PARTICIPATION

In activity participation the hobbyist steadfastly does a kind of leisure that requires systematic physical movement, has inherent appeal, and is pursued within a set of rules. Often the activity poses a challenge, though always a noncompetitive one. When carried out continually for these reasons, the activities included in this type are as diverse as fishing, video games, and barbershop singing.

Folk Art

Folk art is one kind of activity participation. The folk artists have no professional counterpart as amateurs do and so, as a group, have little or no involvement with either professionals or amateurs. Lacking a more suitable term, these enthusiasts have been referred to in serious leisure research as folk artists, for no equivalent appears to exist outside the arts. They should not be confused with the commercial performers or producers of these arts. These performers and producers, as stated in chapter 3, are entertainers. Meanwhile, noncommercial folk artists perform or produce strictly for their own satisfaction and quite often that of other members of the local community, while making their living some other way. They commonly know little about the professional standards of dance, craft, art, music, or theater, although they may unwittingly meet some of them. Having no significant involvement with an amateur-professional system in his or her art, the typical folk artist contributes little or nothing to that system's functioning or to the groups that make it up.

In applying these criteria, it is clear that barbershop singing is a folk art. Nevertheless, the best choral and quartet singing in this idiom does attain high musical and entertainment standards. But they are not professional standards for, as I explain in *The Barbershop Singer*, this art has no professional wing.[5] As in the other folk arts, however, the barbershop public (its audience) is chiefly local, composed mainly of friends and relatives.

Numerically, folk artists are a relatively rare breed. Indeed, given the isolation of most of the rural folk (e.g., Indians, Inuit, hill people), their arts tend to remain hidden from the general public. Even the folk arts of the various urban ethnic groups seem to be largely inaccessible to the uninitiated in the larger community. Still, square dancing, barbershop singing, and morris dancing (a traditional British dance) are not nearly so isolated; depending on the art, they appeal to a certain segment of the general rural or urban public.

Be that as it may, most activity participants seem to prefer one of the other two kinds of hobbies in this subtype: nature activities and corporeal activities.

Nature Activities

This extremely diverse set of interests is pursued in the outdoors. Sorted here into the categories of nature appreciation, nature challenge, and nature exploitation, most are enjoyed most of the time away from towns and cities. Still, within the natural areas in the towns and cities, we may be able to fish, watch birds, cross-country ski, and fly model airplanes, to mention a few possibilities.

Nature Appreciation

At the center of the nature appreciation activities lies the awe-inspiring natural environment in which they take place. Seeing, hearing, smelling, and feeling the surroundings—"getting out in nature"—add up to a powerful reason for doing one or more of the following:

- hiking
- horse riding
- back packing/wilderness camping
- spelunking (cave exploration)[6]
- bird watching

- canoeing/kayaking
- scuba diving/snorkeling
- snowshoeing
- snowmobiling

Another important reason for pursuing these activities is to learn and express the skills and knowledge needed to find fulfillment in them. At this level they are serious leisure.[7]

Nature's Challenges

A nature challenge activity (NCA) is a leisure pursuit whose core activity or activities center on meeting a test posed by the surrounding natural environment. As I have pointed out elsewhere, considerable nature appreciation is also possible in these activities, though at times the challenges are so stiff that they concentrate the mind more or less exclusively on trying to meet them.[8] These activities include:

- ballooning
- flying
- gliding
- wave surfing
- alpine skiing
- snowboarding
- scuba diving
- cross-country skiing
- sailing (with sail/engine)
- parachuting and skydiving
- hang gliding
- mountain climbing
- white water canoeing and kayaking
- dirt (trail) bike riding (noncompetitive)

Thus, an accomplished cross-country skier can savor the beauty of the snow-covered trees and partially frozen streams near trails set on moderate terrain. But then a steep descent with a sharp turn in the middle can suddenly divert all attention to skiing technique.

Nature Exploitation

In these hobbies, if all goes well, participants come away from their sessions in nature with some of its "yield," as experienced in the following:

- fishing
- hunting
- trapping
- mushroom gathering

Yet fishers, hunters, and others do appreciate nature as well, though not when they have a fish on the line or a deer in their sights.

A number of familiar outdoor activities are excluded from these three lists, primarily because they are casual rather than serious leisure (e.g., camping in parks, berry picking, beachcombing). Furthermore, some of the activities just discussed, including sailing, alpine skiing, and cross-country skiing, are sometimes pursued competitively. They are therefore sports and will be considered in the next section as such. Mushroom picking, the sole gathering activity in this list, requires knowing how to identify different species, most crucially the poisonous ones. Unlike berry picking, it is not casual leisure.

Body-Centered Hobbies

The body-centered hobbies draw the participant's attention directly to his or her body. This is in contrast to the nature activities where that person's attention is fixed on an aspect of nature. In the nature activities the body is a vehicle with which to appreciate or exploit nature or meet one of its many challenges. By contrast, routine exercise is a body-centered hobby, though only to the extent it involves skill and knowledge and is considered fulfilling. Swimming, body-building, ice skating, roller skating, and the martial arts (when used for conditioning) number among the exercise activities qualifying as serious leisure.

Gymnastics, tumbling, and acrobatics fall into a separate category of body-centered activity. Although they obviously offer a good deal of exercise, the goal of perfecting a set of difficult bodily maneuvers, or "feats," is equally important. The same may be said for another corporeal activity: ballroom dancing. It, too, provides exercise, while also inspiring its enthusiasts to master such dances as the waltz, foxtrot, samba, rumba, and tango.[9]

Careers in Activity Participation

All the participation activities, when undertaken as serious leisure, call for a significant amount of physical conditioning. A career in this kind of leisure depends on it. Even those who sail, hunt, hike, or watch birds must be fit enough to pursue these interests for at least a couple of hours. Still, some of these activities are less demanding than others. Hang-gliding and fishing from a boat require low levels of conditioning compared with such activities as swimming, gymnastics, and cross-country skiing, in which considerable conditioning is necessary. To the extent that flexibility wanes and bones break more easily in later years, activities like tumbling, gymnastics, alpine skiing, and white-water canoeing are to be avoided at that time of life. Nonetheless, age aside, the many rewards of activity participation as a major type of serious leisure await all who want to be physically active.

As with the making and tinkering hobbies, careers in the activity participation hobbies further unfold along certain distinctive dimensions, two of which are skill and stamina. Both are salient in pursuits like tumbling, wave surfing, roller skating, mountain climbing, cross-country skiing, and ballroom dancing. The number of projects completed is an important dimension for some of these hobbyists, as seen in their lists of important caves explored, notable mountains climbed, or major rivers canoed. The accumulation of knowledge and experience is a prominent fourth dimension in the nature exploitation hobbies. As an example, consider the fishing hobbies, with their rich lore of baits, weather conditions, and feeding habits as it relates to angling for different species of fish.

Social Worlds

With the exception of ballroom dancing and team sailing, literally every participation activity can be pursued alone by people with a taste for solitude. Indeed, many of them can only be pursued alone. Others, among them canoeing, spelunking, backpacking, and hunting, are commonly done with someone else, if for no other reason than for the help and security a partner might provide in emergencies. Whether pursued alone or with others, most participation hobbies have local clubs whose goals include organizing collective outings, serving as repositories of useful information about equipment and nearby sites for pursuing the activity, and holding get-togethers where members can talk shop to their heart's content. Another institution in the social world of some activity participants is the equipment dealer and repair service—the sporting goods store, the backcountry supplier, the wilderness outfitter. Others find their leisure lives organized around certain gyms, pools, rinks, and dance floors. In activity participation, as in so many other forms of serious leisure, the social world of any particular physical activity is encompassing enough to constitute a lifestyle in its own right.

SPORTS, GAMES, AND CONTESTS

The chief difference separating competitors from activity participants is the presence of the most essential component of any sport, game, and contest: interpersonal competition. Both types of hobby are organized according to sets of rules, but in the sports, games, and contests, these rules are always set out in formal terms—in rule books, on printed sheets—designed to control competitive action in (usually) numerous specific ways. The sports are presented here according to their classification as team or individual. Descriptions of each may be found in the larger encyclopedias.

Team Sports

- polo
- curling
- lacrosse
- ringette
- doubles versions of individual sports (e.g., handball, Ping-Pong)

Individual Sports

- darts
- horseshoes
- shuffleboard
- pool/billiards/snooker
- croquet
- handball (singles)
- race walking
- long-distance running
- target, trap, and skeet shooting
- table tennis (Ping-Pong)
- orienteering
- martial arts (e.g., jujitsu, karate, aikido, tae kwon do)

- dog and sled-dog racing
- iceboat racing
- powerboat racing
- model racing (e.g., boats, cars, trains, airplanes)

Orienteering, a sport of Norwegian origin, is a cross-country race on foot guided by map and compass. Ringette is a kind of ice hockey in which a rubber ring is used instead of a puck. Invented in Canada and now played internationally, it is primarily a sport for girls and women, with some of the latter being seniors.[10] Race walking, executed with a special rolling, stiff-legged gait, is distinguished from power walking (exercise) and strolling (casual leisure).

Games

Although the terms *sport* and *game* are frequently interchangeable in common usage, for our purposes it is worth distinguishing the two. The essential differences between them will interest some readers of this book as they search for their optimal leisure lifestyle. A sport is a game based on one or more physical skills, whereas such skills have no place in other games. Further, chance figures heavily in many nonsport games, seen in drawing cards, shaking dice, spinning dials and wheels, and so on. Granted, there are also chance elements in sport games, but they are not an inherent part of the game. In this sense, the nonsport games of chess and checkers resemble sport games.

Since they can never qualify as serious leisure, games based purely on chance (e.g., craps, bingo, roulette) are omitted from the following list. To qualify as serious leisure, an activity must make use of developed skills, knowledge, or experience (or a combination of these three). A game can have chance components and still become a hobby, however, because it also allows decision-making informed by accumulated knowledge of and experience with the game.

Table and board games, dual combat games (e.g., chess, checkers, backgammon)[11]

- money games (e.g., Rich Uncle, Monopoly)
- playing piece games (e.g., Sorry, Parcheesi, Chinese checkers)
- racing games (e.g., Snakes and Ladders)

Card and dice games[12]

- card games for one or two people (e.g., cribbage, gin rummy, the various versions of solitaire)
- card games for three or more playing as individuals (e.g., hearts, poker, rummy, blackjack, canasta)
- card games for three or more playing as a team (e.g., bridge, whist, sheep's head, pinochle)[13]
- craps (dice)[14]

Knowledge and word games

- Scrabble, charades, Pictionary, Trivial Pursuit, among others
- Quizzes[15]

Electronic games

- computer games (video-console games now available on computers—see below)
- video-console games[16]

Role-playing games[17]

- Chivalry & Sorcery
- Dungeons & Dragons
- Empire of the Petal Throne
- Traveller

Miscellaneous games

- backgammon
- dominoes

With the possible exception of the role-playing games, the games listed here need no introduction. Gary Fine, writing in *Shared Fantasy*, describes the role-playing, or fantasy, game as "any game which allows a number of players to assume the roles of imaginary characters and operate with some degree of freedom in an imaginary environment."[18]

Puzzles and Mazes

Because they are noncompetitive, puzzles and mazes designed for leisure purposes are not games in the strictest sense of the definition just set out. More accurately, puzzles and mazes are diversions designed to test the ingenuity, knowledge, or insight of the player. The crossword, acrostic, jigsaw, and mechanical puzzles (e.g., Rubik's Cube) are popular, as are the "brain twisters" like hidden pictures, memory tests, and the mathematical and logical puzzles.[19] They make for interesting leisure for people so inclined.

Leisure Careers

The observations made earlier about physical conditioning and age limitations for activity participants apply with equal validity to the sports mentioned in this section. Furthermore, the sports competitors also have leisure careers similar to those of the activity participants. However, people who play games or solve puzzles follow careers similar to those of some of the collectors and makers and tinkerers. With experience they grow wiser and more sophisticated at playing a particular game or working out a particular puzzle. In addition, puzzle solvers accumulate conquests; they solve a growing number of puzzles, possibly moving up a scale of difficulty as their careers unfold to the point that they enter one of the national or international puzzle contests. As long as the participant's mental acuity holds up, there is no age limit for the games and puzzles, although deteriorating eyesight can certainly discourage participation in them.

Social Worlds

Furthermore, the social worlds of the sports competitors resemble those of the activity participants. The solitary players of games and solvers of puzzles share the condition of aloneness with those activity participants who also cherish it. Indeed, like the puzzle enthusiasts, many of the players going in for solitaire and the electronic games seem to pursue their hobbies virtually alone, beyond a social world of any kind. And the social world of other games players is often minimal, consisting only of those with whom they routinely play (e.g., the wife and husband Scrabble partners, Friday night poker group, and Tuesday morning bridge players). Still, clubs exist in some areas, notably bridge and the role-playing games, and tournaments are now held in bridge, chess, Scrabble, and Monopoly. Absent from the social worlds of most games are the more distant participants like critics, coaches, suppliers, service personnel, and so on, people who enrich the social worlds of many other kinds of serious leisure. Thus, by comparison, the social worlds of many of the puzzlers and game players are simple, which, however, is not to deny that many participants regularly get considerable satisfaction from the social aspects of these hobbies.

THE LIBERAL ARTS HOBBIES

The liberal arts hobbyists are enamored of the systematic acquisition of knowledge for its own sake. Many of them accomplish this by reading voraciously in a field of art (fine and entertainment), sport, cuisine, language, culture, history, science, philosophy, politics, or high-culture fiction and poetry.[20] But some of them go beyond this to expand their knowledge still further through cultural tourism, documentary videos, television programs, and similar resources. These hobbyists look on the knowledge and understanding they gain as an end in itself rather than, as is common in the other serious leisure pursuits, as background or a means to fulfilling involvement in a hobby or an amateur activity. Compared with the other hobbies and the various amateur activities, the knowledge acquired in the liberal arts pastimes is of primary rather than secondary importance.

Though the matter has yet to be studied in detail, it is theoretically possible to separate buffs from consumers in the liberal arts hobbies of sport, cuisine, and the fine and entertainment arts. Some people—call them *consumers*—more or less uncritically consume restaurant fare, sports events, or displays of art (concerts, shows, exhibitions) as pure entertainment and sensory stimulation (casual leisure), whereas others—they are *buffs*—participate in these same situations as more or less knowledgeable experts, as serious leisure. The ever-rarer Renaissance man of our day may also be classified here, even though such people avoid specializing in one field of learning. Instead, their goal is to acquire a somewhat more superficial knowledge of a variety of fields. Being broadly well-read is thus a (liberal arts) hobby of its own.

The liberal arts hobbies are set off from the other serious leisure pursuits by two basic characteristics: the search for broad knowledge of an area of human life and the search for this knowledge for its own sake. Broad knowledge can be compared with technical knowledge—an admittedly fuzzy distinction based on degree rather than on crisp boundaries. Still, we may say that unlike technical, or detailed, knowledge, the broad kind is humanizing.

Through it we can gain a deep understanding and acceptance of a significant sector of human life (art, food, language, history, etc.) and the needs, values, desires, and sentiments found there. Nevertheless, this understanding and acceptance does not necessarily, or even usually, lead to adoption of the sector of life being studied.

Knowledge sought for its own sake implies that its practical application is secondary. Yet liberal arts hobbyists do use the broad knowledge they acquire. For instance, they find considerable satisfaction in expressing this knowledge, and the expression may be an important way for them to maintain and expand it. But this in no way relegates such knowledge to the status of a mere accessory, of being simply a means to a more important end. That is how it often is in the other hobbies and in the amateur and volunteer fields. Here participants need certain kinds of practical information to produce anything of merit.

A third basic characteristic of the liberal arts hobby is the profundity of its broad knowledge; in other words, such knowledge is much more than merely entertaining. This characteristic, which is also found in the more technical bodies of knowledge associated with the other forms of serious leisure, is particularly relevant for the current politics hobbyist. While searching for profound news analyses, this hobbyist must constantly work to avoid, or at least bracket, what David Altheide and Robert Snow refer to as the primarily entertaining and therefore rarely enlightening broadcasts and analyses of the political news heard on radio and television.[21] Entertaining but uninformative mass-media reports and analyses also torment liberal arts hobbyists in the areas of art, sport, and science. Yet the unfortunate lot of many of these enthusiasts is that they often have little choice but to rely on these media for information.

The liberal arts hobbies offer an exceptionally flexible type of serious leisure. They can be carried out at the convenience of the person, molded around other activities (obligatory or not), and accommodated to the demands of work and family. Scheduled courses, lectures, and radio and television programs sometimes momentarily undermine this flexibility. Still, with reading as the main activity, the hobbyist reader's leisure lifestyle is for these reasons unlikely to become too programmed.

In brief, as a genre of leisure, the liberal arts hobbies appeal to a wide segment of the community. In addition, they offer a special place in the world of serious leisure for people bodily unable or psychologically unwilling to pursue more physically demanding activities. Based on the broad appeal and easy financial access of many of these hobbies, they can be accurately described as one of the most, if not *the* most, democratic types of serious leisure.

Hobbyist Reading

In the fine and popular arts this consists for the most part of biographies of famous artists, nontechnical descriptions of how art is produced, its history, its most celebrated expressions (e.g., Leonardo de Vinci's *Mona Lisa*, Beethoven's Fifth Symphony, Rodin's *The Thinker*), and, if available, sociological analyses of the art set in sociocultural context. Hobbyist readers in sport have arguably the largest selection of literature of all the liberal arts hobbies. Accordingly, though we lack data on the matter, it appears that most liberal arts hobbyists in this area are primarily interested in the professional wing. That is, they usually read biographies about professionals (which may include the pros' amateur years), historical accounts of professional sports teams, histories of a certain sport (including its amateur beginnings), chronicles of famous tournaments and playoff series, and possibly other interests. As in art, there is also in liberal arts reading in this field a nontechnical interest in how a given sport is played.

Every culture has its own cuisine, although these days with the globalization of practically everything, all but the most isolated of them has been modified by foreign influences entering as new ingredients, methods of cooking, and ways of preparing food. Liberal arts hobbyists in this area, however, seem not to be interested in every cuisine under the sun, but only in the most celebrated. These are the cuisines for which a voluminous literature, local opportunities to sample public and private exemplars, and a variety of aficionados with whom to talk shop are available. These cuisines are *haute cuisines*, in the sense that none in their *cuisine bourgeoise* form seems to have much hobbyist appeal. In approximate order of greatest interest as a liberal arts hobby, they are French, Italian, Greek, Moroccan/Lebanese, Japanese, Chinese, and Spanish. But, in fact, there is a good deal to read on the cuisine of any major country on the planet. Moreover, in many of these countries, food varies by region, thus giving scope for specialization or, when taken together, a more complex understanding of the cuisine of an entire society.

Learning a language other than one's mother tongue is by its very nature a long-term activity pursued by adults or, at the earliest, older adolescents, as well as by people who have left the ambit of their childhood home and cannot therefore learn the language in question while immersed in the routines of daily life. That is, those learning a second (third, fourth, etc.) language must ordinarily seek some kind of instruction, usually a combination of reading, oral tuition, and face-to-face conversation with other learners and competent speakers. Some of the information gained in these ways, particularly at the beginning of the learner's career in this leisure, is highly practical, centered on vocabulary, grammar, spelling, pronunciation, and so forth. With competence in reading, this liberal arts hobbyist begins to explore various aspects of the culture in which it is embedded—for example, samples of its literature, art, cuisine, and popular activities.

All the liberal arts fields fall under the rubric of culture. That said, some hobbyist readers develop a passion for the culture of a particular country or region. Examples include French Canada, Arabia, Scandinavia, the American West, and the Caribbean. Reading here is necessarily selective in that the full culture of any country or region is too complex and extensive for one person to grasp. Still, some areas appear to be indispensable to a decent general understanding of any culture. These include art, dress, cuisine, history, religion, political system, built environment, and work and leisure, the exploration of which is aided by, at minimum, a tourist's knowledge of the written language.

There seems to be no end to the list of histories that can conceivably attract a committed reading hobbyist. The principal limitation is the amount and accessibility of pertinent material. Assuming that both are sufficient to feed an interest at the hobbyist level, enthusiasts can read passionately about an art, sport, country, military battle, science, industry, technology, religion, ethnic group, or exploratory expedition, to name a few.

Both the liberal arts hobbyists and their amateur counterparts seem mostly attracted to the visible sides of science, to phenomena they can actually or possibly observe without specialized equipment and training. In other words, they tend to avoid fields like chemistry and physics. So hobbyist reading interests in science seem to revolve around phenomena that readers can easily observe locally (amateur astronomers observe locally distant celestial objects).

While liberal arts hobbyists interested in one or more sciences shy away from their theoretical end, those passionate about a philosophy or about the history of philosophy show a different propensity. Philosophy is necessarily abstract, though it should be noted that philosophers usually write about questions of interest to the inquiring mind (e.g., ethics, aesthetics, epistemology, and metaphysics). Hobbyist readers might center their attention on general philosophy, explored by reading an array of books on the subject, some of which contain extracts from the writings of the greats in the field. Others might prefer to specialize in, for instance, moral philosophy or the philosophy of mind, language, or religion. Additional specialties include Western philosophy, Eastern philosophy, medieval philosophy, modern philosophy, and ancient philosophy. Then there are the philosophical schools of existentialism, pragmatism, phenomenology, German idealism, and so on.

The reading buffs in politics, who may well be partisan, are nonetheless in constant search of the most reputable, up-to-date reports and analyses of political events. Our definition of politics is that of the *New Shorter Oxford English Dictionary*: "Public life and affairs involving the authority and government of a State or part of a State." As a liberal arts hobby, this involves regularly reading, for the most part, books and periodicals respected for their reportorial accuracy and analytic acumen. The ordinary, popular news media, described earlier in this chapter as basically entertainment, are commonly avoided. They are regarded as too often inaccurate and their analyses as too often questionable or unconvincing.

Elsewhere I have labeled as *belletrists* those who make a hobby of reading fine-art, high-culture fiction and poetry, as well as its criticism.[22] Belletristic literature is the product of creative writing and its analysis. Of all the kinds of reading covered in this section on the liberal arts hobbies, belletristic fiction and poetry is where buffs are least inclined to speed read.

Belletrists read slowly and carefully, doing so for several reasons. One of them is that they want to devour with relish the artistry of the writing. To do this, they dissect the text of the novel or poem, reveling in the words, sentences, and figures of speech of the author, but pondering as well how these creations might be different. In belletristic fiction the reader mulls over the plot and subplots, contemplating their intricacy, trying to anticipate how they will unfold, marveling at the imaginative way each has been constructed, and the like. Belletrists also give considerable thought to the characters in the work, to the author's description of them, their relationships with each other, their fit within the plot, and so forth.

Social World

And what may we say about the social world of the liberal arts hobbyist? People learning a new language, who hope to become fluent in it, must enter in a profound way the social world of the people already fluent in the language. Yet language as a liberal arts hobby associated with a well-developed social world is the exception. So far as is known in serious leisure research, the other liberal arts hobbies have at best only weakly developed social worlds. They are often social, to be sure, but the manner of pursuing these hobbies is generally personal, centered primarily in reading alone and secondarily in viewing and listening. The closest most liberal arts hobbyists typically come to entering a social world is when, to advance their interests, they take a noncredit course or participate in an educational travel program. Some join book clubs or discussion groups. Some go to author readings or hang out at book fairs. Yet their core activity is reading, of necessity a solitary interest. The liberal arts hobby of historical reenactment is an exception, for enthusiasts here express their knowledge of key events in the past by theatrically reenacting them in the present and doing so within a social world of enormous complexity.[23]

GETTING STARTED IN A HOBBY

We begin with collecting and move from there to making and tinkering; participation in activities; competing in games, sports, and contests; and pursuing the liberal arts hobbies. One general hint for getting started in a hobby is to search for relevant books and periodicals in the public libraries as well as the larger bookstores and magazine outlets in the community. And here as elsewhere, the Internet is a wonderful source of information. More specific advice pertaining to each type of hobby is presented below.

Collecting

The first move in acquiring the object in question is obvious in the collection of natural objects. In other kinds of collecting the collector typically begins by exploring the shops selling stamps, antiques, coins and currency, or paintings and sculptures. Prints and posters are sold in such places as gift and souvenir shops and the picture framing services. Furthermore, collectors soon learn from colleagues in the hobby, and perhaps from clerks in the shops, about the existence of shows, auctions, and good-quality mail-order services. Those same clerks may also be able to direct the beginner to a local, regional, or national club or association concerned with a particular kind of collecting; these groups are especially likely to emerge around art, guns, toys, stamps, old cars, and coins and currency.

Making and Tinkering

As in collecting, getting started in the making and tinkering hobbies is rarely a mystery. Most people who want to learn to cook or make wine or beer would think to enroll in one or more classes offered by either a continuing education program or a related business (e.g., wine shop, kitchen supply store). It is the same for the decorative activities—the leather and textile crafts, the interlacing and interlocking activities, and some of the miscellaneous crafts, especially candle making and mosaic making—except that the related businesses are the local craft shops. In the same vein, some of the hobby shops and continuing education programs offer the occasional set of classes for budding toy and model makers. Not to be forgotten are the how-to books, which are available for all the making and tinkering hobbies. In some of these hobbies, notably do-it-yourself and wood, metal, and lapidary work, the books are the main learning resource, since classes are relatively uncommon. The public library often carries many of these. Finally, the social world of each of these hobbies has its commercial equipment and supplies sector (e.g., the craft shop, hardware store, fabric outlet), where advice is readily available from experienced practitioners and pertinent how-to literature (including books) is sold or distributed free of charge.

Organized hobbyist spaces exist in North America, which have been established for making a wide variety of things. Known as "hackerspace" or "hackspacc" (other names include "hacklab," "makerspace," or "creative space"), they serve as places where people with common interests may gather to socialize, collaborate, and, above all, make something. Often the interests center on computers, technology, science, digital art, and electronic art. Wikipedia describes *hackerspaces* as open community labs, where one finds many of the tools of the machine shop and workshop. Other spaces resemble more a studio. In any case, "hackers" gather here to share resources and knowledge and to build and make things. These places are often located in social centers, adult education centers, public schools, university campuses, or "infoshops," and there is frequently free software, open hardware, and alternative media.[24]

Activity Participation

The first category of activity participation discussed in chapter 3 was the folk arts, of which only barbershop singing and square dancing were said to be generally accessible. Both require training to participate, although the vast majority of barbershop choruses (in which most people start) accept singers who can pass a handful of simple voice tests. It is often difficult, however, to find the local chapter of Harmony Incorporated or Sweet Adelines International, both female organizations, or that of the Barbershop Harmony Society (formerly the Society for the Preservation and Encouragement of Barbershop Quartet Singing in America, or SPEBSQSA), a male organization. Since each chapter's name is unique, it is next to impossible to find it in the telephone directory, if even listed there. But this problem is quickly solved by visiting these organizations online, where you may obtain the name of the local chorus and the name and telephone number of its contact person. Life is easier for beginning square dancers, for they need only locate the continuing education programs that offer classes in this hobby or the clubs that organize it (see the yellow pages).

Courses exist for virtually every participation activity that challenges nature. Given where geographically appropriate (e.g., mountaineering courses near the mountains, surfing courses near the sea), they may last no more than a day or two or as long as two years or more. For example, balloonists must be certified (see the yellow pages heading "Balloons-Manned") and pilots of planes and gliders must be licensed (see the yellow pages under "Aircraft Schools"). Lengthy training is also necessary for parachuting and scuba diving (see the yellow pages). In fact, a sizable majority of the people meeting one of nature's challenges as a hobby appear to start out with some kind of formal instruction.

By contrast, notwithstanding the sporadic availability of classes, most enthusiasts of nature exploitation—fishing, hunting, trapping, mushroom gathering—seem to enter their hobby by way of informal instruction from friends or relatives. The routes to the nature appreciation hobbies are the most varied. It appears that rather few people take classes in hiking, snowshoeing, bird watching, snowmobiling, or horseback riding (as opposed to the equestrian events), another set of activities mostly approached informally through friends and relatives. This may also be true for spelunking. But many people take noncredit classes in skin diving or canoeing through a college or university department of leisure or physical education. In all the participation activities there is no shortage of books and magazines reporting on how and where to do them. Depending on the activity, look for readings as well as expert advice in sporting goods stores, fishing and hunting shops, backcountry outfitters, and equestrian suppliers. Finally, remember to check the relevant holdings in the public library.

Adults entering the body-centered activities of swimming and gymnastics for routine exercise usually take classes at a public or private pool or gym. By contrast, ice skating, roller skating (including inline skating), and body building are often learned on one's own, perhaps with a modicum of advice from a friend or relative. Body building is often undertaken at the YMCA, the YWCA, or one of the other "Health Studios" (yellow pages classification). Note, too, that classes in these activities are sometimes available through one of the continuing education programs.

Sports, Games, and Contests

Nearly all the team and individual sports considered in this section can be played with at least minor satisfaction after a modicum of on-the-spot instruction from an experienced player. The exceptions to this generalization are polo and the martial arts, two sports with required conditioning and background skills that obviate immediate participation. Otherwise, entry is comparatively easy, provided the beginner can find someone to impart the rudiments of the sport and indicate the places where one may compete in it. Apart from reading a book on the sport in question, the strategy mentioned earlier of hanging around the scene is a common way to become involved (e.g., pool rooms, race tracks, playing fields). Watch for notices of competitions in the sections of the newspaper devoted to sports and community events. Moreover, the players of some of these sports are organized in clubs (see the yellow pages under "Clubs"), and there may be a continuing education program offering classes in some of them. Finally, beginners may sometimes start their own scene by purchasing a dart set, croquet set, or pool table and inviting friends in for a game or two.

This latter strategy for becoming involved is more universally applicable to the various games designed for two or more players. In other words, beginners may establish bridge or poker groups or set up with interested partners regular playing sessions of chess, Scrabble, Monopoly, or gin rummy. Alternatively, a would-be player can get started in bridge through a continuing education class. If the role-playing games have appeal, search for a club devoted to one or more of them. Since these clubs are common on university campuses, ask the office of the student president for information about them. Finally, note that some of the games, such as charades and Pictionary, make good party activities because they can involve everyone present.

The remaining games and all the puzzles are easy to learn and enjoyed alone. The beginner need only switch on the video or computer and follow instructions, shuffle the cards and deal a hand of solitaire, or read the instructions and start to work the puzzle.

The Liberal Arts Hobbies

With few exceptions, participants in the liberal arts hobbies also pursue their leisure as a solitary activity. For this reason a beginner seldom needs much advice on how to get started. Since reading is the main way of learning in these hobbies, he or she simply starts exploring the relevant sections of the community's libraries, bookstores, magazine stands, and online equivalents with the goal of building the broad, profound, nontechnical knowledge so highly prized by this type of hobbyist. Novices should also be alert for material with which to augment their reading, particularly public talks and audio and video documentaries.

And, for the participant who can afford them, trips taken as part of an educational travel program can also significantly augment knowledge and understanding in the geographically based liberal arts hobbies. A number of universities have noncredit, educational travel programs. They are similar to the Road Scholar/Elderhostel Program, which is composed of one- to three-week noncredit courses presently offered in over 150 countries. It and the university educational travel programs exemplify touristic, self-directed education in the liberal arts. The Road Scholar/Elderhostel program holds special appeal for people over sixty years old, the minimum age of eligibility. In addition to these programs, there are available on the Internet nearly countless cultural tours and culturally related camps and workshops. The private tour companies round out the cultural touring possibilities for the liberal arts hobbyist (see online and, in the yellow pages, explore "Travel Service" and similar headings).

Unlike the other liberal arts hobbyists, people learning a new language who hope to advance to a level at which they can easily read and talk in it must participate in a profound way in one of the social worlds of the people fluent in that tongue. Consequently, entering this hobby is anything but a solitary activity. I reported in a study of Anglophones desiring to learn French that they began by taking noncredit language courses offered by Berlitz Languages, a continuing education program, or a college or university department of French.[25] Once their linguistic fluency improved sufficiently, some of the students deepened their involvement in the local Francophone social world by frequenting its clubs, bookstores, cinemas, restaurants, travel agencies, and festivals and special events. In turn, these contacts engendered a small but expanding number of French-language friendships, acquaintances, and network connections. For some, those same contacts also led to opportunities to work as volunteers for one or two of the Francophone services in their community. Other students with the time and financial means achieved the same end by participating in a local Francophone social world elsewhere in, say, Quebec or France.

POSITIVE SIMPLICITY IN THE HOBBIES

As it is with the amateur activities, so it is with the hobbies: some cost a lot, some are moderately expensive, and some may be classified as nonconsumptive leisure. At the expensive end of this dimension lie the collections of art objects, coins and currency, and antiques; the raising and breeding of certain animals, plants, and trees (e.g., horses, fruit orchards); and such participant activities as scuba (costly equipment and travel to sites), ballooning, flying, gliding, and big-game hunting and fishing. Polo and powerboat racing head the list of the dearest activities in the sports field. Whereas this is not an exhaustive list of the most expensive hobbies, its shortness nevertheless conveys a message: the hobbies are mostly an affordable set of activities for a reasonably large segment of the population.

Thus there is available plenty of nonconsumptive hobbyist leisure. The liberal arts hobbies may be described as such, to the extent that readers use libraries, borrow reading material from others, and buy cheap electronic or hard copies of used books. It is the same for collecting natural objects and for some of the paper crafts (e.g., scrapbooking, origami, and papier-mâché). Nonconsumptive participant activities include bird watching (after the initial purchase of binoculars for those who want them), mushroom picking (need a basket), and "low-tech" hiking (should have decent footwear). Finally, in the category of games, negligible money is put out for a deck of cards or pair of dice, and the role-playing games cost nothing to participate in. The rest—the vast majority of the hobbies—are moderately expensive, with some of these being basically nonconsumptive once the initial cost of equipment is met (e.g., purchase of a board game, microscope, or croquet set). Some hobbies require their enthusiasts to join a club or organization that provides an essential service like a gym, ice rink, swimming pool, or dance floor. This may be the most costly part of the activities pursued there.

The positive simplistic measures to consider when searching for and adopting a hobby are the same as those set out at the end of the preceding chapter for the amateur activities. No need to repeat them here.

Chapter Five

Volunteering

> I don't know what your destiny will be, but one thing I do know: the only ones among you who will be really happy are those who have sought and found how to serve.
>
> Albert Schweitzer

Volunteering: Is it work, leisure, neither of these, or a separate category—that is, just plain volunteering? Although my research indicates that some people have trouble answering this question, making a case for volunteering as leisure actually poses little logical difficulty. If the word "volunteering" is to remain consistent with its French and Latin roots, it, along with all other leisure, may only be seen as chosen activity, as activity people *want* to do. Moreover, as with other leisure, volunteering may only be seen as either a fulfilling or a pleasurable, positive experience. Otherwise, we are forced to conclude that the so-called volunteers of this kind are somehow pushed into performing their roles by circumstances they would prefer to avoid, which is a contradiction of terms.

Fulfilling and *rewarding* have been used from the beginning of this book to describe the overall experience of the serious pursuits. They are better descriptors for them than the more common terms "pleasurable" and "enjoyable." Indeed, the latter pair were said in chapter 2 to describe best what we get from casual leisure, including, as will be discussed shortly, casual volunteering. This is, in more concrete language, what Schweitzer means by being "really happy" through serving others.

Note further that, whereas it is true that volunteers are paid in rare instances, even beyond the expenses they incur, these emoluments are much too small to constitute a livelihood or obligate the person in some way. Finally, it is also true that volunteering normally includes the clear requirement of being in a particular place at a specified time to carry out an assigned function. But, as we have already seen with reference to amateurs and hobbyists, some serious leisure may also involve such obligations to some extent, though generally not to the extent typical of work.

WHAT IS VOLUNTEERING?

Volunteering is uncoerced, intentionally productive, altruistic activity engaged in during free time. Engaged in as leisure, it is thus activity that people want to do.[1] Moreover, using their abilities and resources, they actually do it in either an enjoyable (casual leisure) or a fulfilling (serious leisure) way (sometimes both).

This definition alludes to the two principal motives behind volunteering. One is helping others—volunteering as altruism. The other is helping oneself—volunteering as self-interestedness. Examples of the latter include working for a strongly felt cause or working to experience, as serious leisure enthusiasts do everywhere, the variety of social and personal rewards available in volunteering and the leisure career in which they are framed. In other words, this is an inwardly rewarding self-interestedness. It is one driven by a desire to reach such externally based advantages as gaining work experience to facilitate getting a job or filling a requirement in a training program.

Thus what marks leisure volunteering as a special type of serious leisure is its altruism. A significant part of what is rewarding about volunteering is the benign regard for another person or a set of others as manifested in and communicated through particular acts and activities. By contrast, altruism is largely absent in the other two types of serious leisure. More precisely, altruistic action is, in reality, volunteer work done as a sideline to the person's amateur or hobbyist interest.

That we may have a (leisure) career as a volunteer has given birth to the distinction between *career volunteering*, the serious leisure form, and *casual volunteering*. In this regard, it appears that the motive of self-interestedness drives the pursuit of career volunteering more than the motive of altruism. This holds even in times when our altruism inspired us to enter the field in the first place. A major reason for this difference is that career volunteering involves acquiring, over time, certain skills, knowledge, or training (and, not infrequently, all three of these). Their acquisition contributes to the sense of an evolving career, itself highly rewarding. As Coralie McCormack and her colleagues summed up for female baby boomers who were seeking this kind of volunteering in retirement, "I want to do more than just cut the sandwiches."[2]

WHAT VOLUNTEERS DO

Volunteering often carries with it a clear obligation to be at a particular place at a specified time to perform a certain function. Yet career volunteering seems to engender no greater load of commitments than many other serious leisure pursuits. For example, serious leisure participants can be obligated to attend rehearsals and perform in the next concert of the community orchestra, play for their team in an upcoming game in the local industrial baseball league, or, as career volunteers, go to the neighborhood primary school at four o'clock two days a week to help children with their reading problems.

Moreover, as with other types of serious leisure, career volunteering brings on the occasional need to persevere. Participants who want to continue experiencing the same level of satisfaction in the activity have to meet certain challenges from time to time. Thus, musicians must practice assiduously to master difficult musical passages, baseball players must throw repeatedly to perfect their favorite pitches, and volunteers must search their imaginations for new approaches with which to help children with reading problems. Perseverance can also help volunteers realize such rewards as self-actualization and self-expression. It happens in all three types of serious leisure that the deepest rewards sometimes come at the *end* of the activity, rather than *during* it.

Volunteers serving in an organization usually perform tasks delegated to them by a superior. This person is normally either a managerial employee or a senior volunteer in the same organization. Superiors give out tasks that they believe volunteers can do, given adequate training and experience; that staff believe are beyond their jurisdiction; or, given budgetary limitations, that staff cannot take on themselves.

Such arrangements turn these volunteers into outsiders in agencies and work organizations otherwise composed of insiders. Indeed, the volunteers' expertise and competence may even threaten some insiders. All of this indicates that organizational volunteers are neither facsimiles of professionals, as amateurs are, nor bureaucratized workers. Instead, they are often a special class of helper in someone else's occupational world.

Finally, retirees who are volunteering may observe while "on the job" that some of their leisure-time colleagues don't quite fit the definition just set out. The retirees may be trying to understand the "marginal volunteers" in their midst. The marginal volunteer "feels significant moral coercion to agree to do something. Depending on the activity, a certain range of choice of activity is available to the volunteer, but choice that is nonetheless guided substantially by extrinsic interests or pressures, by influential forces lying outside the volunteer activity itself."[3] Marginal volunteering is exemplified by extracurricular activities in the workplace and exploratory volunteering in search of a work career. There is, in this kind of volunteering, a certain feeling of being coerced to engage in the volunteer activity.

THE SCOPE OF VOLUNTEERING

The following list of areas of volunteer work shows the enormous scope of this kind of leisure, which touches virtually every aspect of everyday life. One way to demonstrate this scope is to look at what interests motivate people to volunteer. I have observed elsewhere that our volunteer activities are motivated, in part, by one of six types of interest: those involving (1) people, (2) ideas, (3) things, (4) flora, (5) fauna, or (6) the natural environment.[4] Each type, or combination of types, offers its volunteers an opportunity to pursue, through an altruistic activity, a particular kind of interest. Thus, volunteers interested in promoting a religion or political philosophy like idea-based volunteering, whereas those interested in preserving certain kinds of animals (fish or birds) like faunal volunteering. These interests may be pursued as serious, casual, or project-based leisure.

These six types of interests are, however, rather general. Many people prefer to channel their volunteering toward a particular sector of community life. Here they seek careers in serious leisure volunteering through either formal activity—working within an organization or association—or informal activity—working with friends or neighbors, or working with a small group such as a club or self-help group. Some volunteer careers combine both types. These sectors also offer abundant opportunity for casual and project-based volunteering, which will be discussed in the next chapter. I consider eighteen sectors below.

Community Services

Most volunteering opportunities are of the service variety; the volunteers usually offer needed assistance to a particular set of people. Sometimes, however, it is not people who are served, but rather an ideology, an environmental feature, or a physical object. This is evident in, respectively, volunteering to help promote a religion, clean up a river, and save an old building. Moreover, for career volunteers eager for some responsibility, there are managerial posts—for example, team captain of a unit of volunteer firefighters or coordinator of volunteers in a residence for the elderly. Along these same lines, a small number of volunteer workers wind up in decision-making positions as members of boards of directors or executive committees.

Bear in mind that simple membership in a club or voluntary association is not in itself volunteering, not even casual volunteering. Being on a membership list is not an activity. Members who regularly attend meetings can be considered volunteers, however, to the extent that they participate actively in the group's affairs. Whether their volunteering is of the career variety or the casual variety depends on the nature of their participation. The secretary and treasurer are most certainly career volunteers, whereas the rank and file who regularly attend the meetings—but have only a superficial interest in the issues discussed on the floor—are best regarded as casual volunteers.

Mary Kouri has identified seventeen areas of volunteering, which together demonstrate the immense spread of this kind of leisure.[5] The Internet addresses of the national and international organizations mentioned in this section are available in the "Resources" section at the back of this book or, occasionally, as a reference in the endnotes for this chapter. Their local branches, if any, may be found in a community's yellow pages or else online using the title of the organization as the search term.

Necessities

The necessities provided are food, shelter, clothing, and other basic goods and services. Local food banks, the Goodwill Industries, and the Salvation Army number among the organizations using volunteers to serve the poor. Some volunteers provide these necessities by collecting used clothing and household items, some repair these items once collected, and some distribute the restored items to the needy. Other volunteers work in hostels and missions providing shelter to the homeless. Volunteers also prepare the meals served to the indigent or deliver meals to a home-bound clientele through the Meals on Wheels organization.

Education

Some educational volunteers work under a teacher's supervision, tutoring students with problems in such areas as reading, spelling, and mathematics. Alternatively, these volunteers help organize and run field trips and extracurricular activities (see the National Association of Partners in Education, Inc.).[6] To the extent that it is substantial and enduring, work for the school's Parent Teacher Association (PTA) may also be considered educational volunteering of the serious or casual variety. Additionally, people skilled in a foreign language are sometimes invited to help students polish their linguistic accents, oral delivery, and reception of the tongue, a kind of service that includes teaching immigrants English as a second language. Organizations such as ProLiteracy—formed in 2002 from Literacy Volunteers of America and Laubach Literacy Action—have the goal of promoting competence in English for all.[7] Volunteers are welcome here as language tutors. And a volunteer, most commonly a parent, occasionally augments the coaching staff of one of the school's interscholastic sports. In some communities, the school bus drivers work gratis and volunteers with sufficient background are used to instruct school dropouts in trade skills like printing, textile work, woodworking, and metal work. Volunteers are also needed to teach the repair of the many items of equipment used in these areas and several others, as well as the repair of the products turned out there. Finally, volunteer teachers may be invited to instruct in the repair of textiles, paper products (e.g., books), and products made of sand, glass, stone, and clay.

Science

Scientific volunteers sometimes collaborate with schools where they help organize and run science fairs and long-term classroom projects in the physical and biological sciences. Others are amateurs converted into volunteer public relations officers for their sciences, as seen in their efforts to educate the general public in the fundamentals of the discipline. They may also lobby the government for favorable legislation. Additionally, volunteers are contracted as guides to serve in such establishments as zoos, museums, arboretums, planetariums, and botanical gardens. Finally, they may be given specific volunteer tasks in certain scientific research projects. In this capacity, they fill the role of assistant, thereby distinguishing themselves from the more autonomous amateur scientists mentioned earlier. The Earthwatch Institute, an international service with offices in many parts of the world, organizes such help for a number of these projects. Its mission is to recruit volunteers to work in professional research in art, archaeology, and marine studies, as well as in the geosciences, life sciences, and social sciences.

Civic Affairs

Civic affairs cover an extremely broad area, even though it excludes politics, a separate field considered below. In general, volunteering in civic affairs entails working in a community-level service or project, most probably one sponsored by government. For instance, volunteers are recruited for certain municipal services, including governmentally run historical sites, an assortment of special projects (e.g., World's Fair, Olympic Games, major arts festivals), and the many programs in tourism and sports and fitness. Here volunteers serve as tour guides, staff visitor information booths, and work in programs for youth or seniors. They are also invited (usually as casual leisure participants) to help maintain tourist sites and public grounds. Some civic affairs volunteers find work at the public library, while others become involved in neighborhood crime or fire prevention. Those with appropriate skills and experience may be asked to write brochures, historical material, or even technical documents. The branches of municipal government with the greatest need for volunteers are, first, the one concerned with parks, leisure, and recreation, and, second, the one responsible for social services.

Spiritual Development

Spiritual development refers to lay religious counseling and education, an area as diverse as the many religions available in the modern world. Friendly visiting at times of death, disaster, or severe illness exemplify this sort of volunteering. Missionary work belongs here, as well, to the extent that it is fulfilling and neither coerced nor substantially remunerated. Teaching Christian Sunday school (or its equivalent in other religions) and leading adult discussion groups also contribute to spiritual development. Most opportunities for volunteering in this area appear to come through a religious organization, either one associated with a religious movement or with an established religion.

Religion

The volunteer activities covered in this section are centered not on spiritual development, discussed above, but rather on the actual running of religious organizations. Here there is great variety. Volunteers in this area are recruited to organize and run social events and charity campaigns, as well as fill lay roles in religious services. Many churches are organized, in part, according to committees, all of which are staffed mainly, if not entirely, with volunteers. In addition, volunteers are used extensively to distribute literature and disseminate information about their religion. They work in religion-specific information centers (e.g., Christian Science Reading Rooms), staff telephone information lines, and hand out brochures and booklets. A fruitful way to find volunteer opportunities in religion is to search the websites of local churches, mosques, synagogues, and the like. The entries in the online edition of the yellow pages often include a link to the websites of the religious organizations listed there.

Health

Volunteer work in health is restricted by the jurisdictional controls of such professions as nursing and medicine. Nonetheless, volunteers with appropriate certification are engaged to teach first-aid courses and present public lectures on health-related issues. In hospitals and private homes, they feed people who have trouble feeding themselves; provide company for lonely patients by way of reading and conversation; and work to retrain the temporarily disabled by helping them swim, walk, and otherwise move their atrophied limbs. Despite these many services, health volunteers are possibly most active in the physical fitness arena, where they guide exercise sessions in yoga, aerobics, and similar activities. Finally, these volunteers are needed for work with the mentally disordered and physically disabled to help them adapt to life in the wider community. Some provide transportation for these people using specially designed vehicles. Relevant American and worldwide organizations include the Senior Corps, Red Cross, and American Association of People with Disabilities (which utilizes volunteer mentors), in addition to a sizable number of disease-specific organizations concerned with cancer, heart disease, Alzheimer's, and the like.

Economic Development

Opportunities for volunteering in this area are nearly innumerable. For one, volunteers fill diverse roles in the many organizations providing help or relief in the developing world. In this regard, some volunteers solicit money for CARE or Oxfam, whereas others serve as clerks, managers, or secretaries in these organizations. Some American volunteers go overseas with the Peace Corps to work directly with local people by, for example, helping them build a school or an irrigation system or establish an effective nutritional program. People with the appropriate training may find it satisfying to work abroad for Volunteers in Overseas Cooperative Assistance (VOCA) or Global Volunteer Network (GVN). Back home, volunteers with an entrepreneurial background—often retirees—advise on ways to get new businesses off the ground or help those that are floundering to survive (e.g., Service Corps of Retired Executives). Volunteers in Service to America (now called AmeriCorps VISTA) work to revitalize low-income rural, urban, and Native American individuals and their communities.

Natural Environment

Some people in this area volunteer to enhance public lands, lakes, and streams by, for example, planting trees or caring for lawns and flower gardens. Others devote their after-work time to improving the execution of an outdoor activity such as by cleaning up beaches, beautifying picnic grounds, clearing hiking and skiing trails, or removing refuse and deadfall from trout streams. Sports and environmentalist groups (e.g., the Sierra Club) rely heavily on volunteers to conduct publicity campaigns about their programs and concerns, as well as to try to persuade the government to stop certain practices inimical to the environment or a particular outdoor sport. One major consumer of volunteer time in this area is the volunteer program of the United States Department of Agriculture, Forest Service.[8] The American Hiking Society does similar work through its Volunteer Vacations program. Volunteers also teach in state or provincially run programs designed to impart to youth outdoor skills and responsible use of natural resources. Finally, the National Wildlife Federation offers a vast array of volunteer possibilities revolving around the welfare of nature's creatures and their habitat.

Politics

It appears that most volunteers in politics work for a political party. Their duties include disseminating information about its platform and candidates by carrying banners, posting notices, canvassing door to door, and distributing party literature. These people are joined by other volunteers at local meetings of the party where they choose election candidates, hammer out campaign strategies, and organize publicity drives. Moreover, it tends to fall to volunteers to bring new members into the party and raise funds for its operation. Finally, some of the most faithful and committed party members are elected as delegates to state, provincial, and national conventions.

Outside the framework of the political parties lie hundreds of special-interest groups, entities run almost entirely by volunteers.[9] They are political inasmuch as they hope either to change government policy or to preserve the status quo. More broadly, organizations in the United States like Common Cause strive to ensure good government (volunteer as a lobbyist), while voters' organizations at the state level, along with the League of Women Voters (link to a local league for volunteer needs) and, in Canada, the Canadian Women's Voters Congress, work through volunteers to generate maximum voter participation at the polls. In all these groups, the appetite for help in lobbying the government and informing the voters is nearly insatiable. Still another type of political volunteering is that done for such organizations as the American Civil Liberties Union and the Canadian Civil Liberties Association.

Note that all this is about political volunteering in democratic societies, which, however, amount to a minority of all the world's nations. The *Economist* Intelligence Unit's Index of Democracy 2010 reveals that 12.3 percent of the world's population (15.6 percent of all countries) lives in a "full democracy." Another 37.2 percent (31.7 percent of all countries) lives in a "flawed democracy."[10] Of all the volunteer activities discussed in this chapter, those of the political volunteer are geographically the most restricted.

Government

Volunteers here work in programs and services run by a branch of a municipal, county, state, provincial, or federal government. Volunteer firefighters and emergency service workers (in, for example, first aid, disaster relief, and search and rescue) exemplify voluntary action in this area. Furthermore, some urban police forces are using volunteers to staff citizen patrols and operate neighborhood crime-prevention programs.[11] Volunteers are also widely employed in the entire range of government-run youth and seniors' programs. Additionally, some judicial systems recruit volunteers to work with parolees, as well as provide various kinds of assistance in courtrooms.

Safety

This is the classificatory home of those volunteers who work to prevent violence and disorderly conduct in the schools and on the playgrounds. Adult school-patrol guards constitute another example, as do groups formed to prevent bullying on educational sites. More generally, the Guardian Angels have emerged as a nonviolent volunteer organization dedicated to restoring order to urban streets and transportation systems in many of the larger cities around the world. This community-wide manifestation of safety volunteering, founded in 1979 in New York, now has one hundred thirty chapters operating in seventeen countries.

Human Relationships

This area embraces the volunteer work centered on establishing and maintaining a long-term relationship between a child and an adult, or between two adults. Examples include the ties established through the exchange-student programs linking students with their host families and through the youth programs linking troubled adolescents with adult mentors. Mentoring, which is sometimes confused with coaching and consultation, is most accurately seen as a kind of informal volunteering.[12] Volunteers serving in the programs of Big Brothers and Big Sisters International (now active in thirteen countries) develop similar ties with their clients. The welcoming programs for new residents are organized around the formation of interpersonal relationships between newcomers to the community and established local residents. Finally, a variety of social services are provided by volunteers working closely with individual clients over a period of time. These services are delivered in such places as women's shelters, centers for runaway teenagers, and halfway houses and reintegration programs for reforming alcoholics, drug users, and newly released prisoners. Other volunteer services of this type are made available through parental-aid programs and aid programs for children and seniors.

The Arts

This area of volunteering centers primarily on the needs of local and regional arts groups. Groups in dance, music, and theater often need help in making costumes, constructing sets, writing programs, and publicizing performances. These groups are amateur, by and large, since the professionals tend to rely on paid equivalents. Still, some amateur groups and many professional groups are governed by volunteer boards of directors. Furthermore, there is a voracious appetite for volunteers to help with the operation of the various annual arts festivals, the planning and execution of which span much of the year. The individual arts of painting and craft work, for example, although less dependent on volunteers than the collective arts, nevertheless routinely solicit their help in publicizing and staffing exhibitions and in writing the materials announcing their dates and locations.

National Public Radio (NPR), at its headquarters in Washington, D.C., recruits volunteers to answer its telephones, operate its computers, prepare mailings, post newspaper clippings, and organize and conduct tours of its facilities. Volunteers also represent NPR at various cultural events throughout the country. Thus, most volunteering at NPR is organized at and according to the needs of its local radio stations. They may be reached through the online yellow pages of a particular city using the search term "public radio." What usually turns up is a street address and telephone number. Alternatively, look up their website.

Recreation

Some of the activities of recreational volunteers were covered earlier under the headings of education, government, and civic affairs. Beyond these spheres, this type of volunteer can be found organizing and running events at the different sports clubs and unaffiliated annual sports competitions so common these days in running, cycling, canoe racing, and cross-country ski racing, to mention a few.[13] Adult volunteers serve as referees for most child and adolescent sports contests, and even some involving adults. Elsewhere, volunteer recreational workers perform a diversity of functions at many of the summer camps for children and adolescents. Those who work with the Boy Scouts, Girl Scouts, and similar organizations are, for the most part, recreational volunteers. In addition, there are volunteers who work with children as storytellers. Finally, the volunteer ushers for plays, games, shows, and concerts form another significant part of this group.

Organizational Support Services

The large majority of volunteer activities considered so far are formal; each is carried out within the framework of at least one organization or association. Moreover, running an organization is itself a complicated and time-consuming undertaking in which volunteers can fill a variety of important support roles. Thus, in all these areas, volunteer help is also routinely sought for clerical and secretarial functions. In many areas, a need also exists for bookkeeping and accounting services, a support activity qualified volunteers often provide. To the extent that the activity is managed and administered outside of a private home, a volunteer may be engaged to do janitorial work or maintain the grounds around the building.

Informal Volunteering

To qualify as serious leisure, informal volunteer work for friends or neighbors must be regular and substantial. Regularly volunteering to babysit a child, care for a pet, clean a friend's house, or do a neighbor's yard work are some current examples. Participating regularly and substantially in the affairs of a small club or self-help group is a well-known form of informal volunteering, as is working with one of the "anonymous" groups—Debtors Anonymous, Gamblers Anonymous, Neurotics Anonymous, Alcoholics Anonymous, and so on. Furthermore, a number of small clubs and societies engage in informal volunteering, usually as part of a broader mission. They offer a specialized service such as cleaning up roadsides, helping needy children, or developing and disseminating views on, say, the uses of or policies about a nearby park, lake, or river. Local chapters of the Society for the Prevention of Cruelty to Animals (SPCA), or its localized equivalents, offer an opportunity for informal volunteering by people concerned about the welfare of urban pets.

CAREER VOLUNTEERING

It is impossible to list every kind of volunteering found in any one of these areas. The different kinds are simply too numerous to include in this book. Moreover, new ways of volunteering are emerging at an accelerating rate, as the effects of electronic technology are felt ever more widely throughout societies everywhere. Nevertheless, the wide scope of volunteering in North America is clearly evident in the foregoing sections and should provide anyone interested in a particular category with a sufficient understanding of the kinds of volunteering available there to proceed with his or her own search. That search will be greatly aided by the suggestions presented in the "Resources" section.

Some of the areas of career volunteering considered in this chapter require significant amounts of training. Indeed some, including many in education, require full certification of the volunteer, even though this person is working without pay. Obviously, these areas are open only to specialists who have retired or who find their volunteering too exciting to abandon in their free time after work. Yet it is fortunate that entry into the large majority of the aforementioned activities is substantially less restrictive.

It is also obvious that some of the activities just discussed lend themselves to either casual involvement or serious involvement, depending on the activities offered to the volunteer. For instance, a clear difference exists between the ability and experience required to coordinate a canoe race consisting of scores of contestants and that required to ensure that each pair of paddlers is properly registered. The first exemplifies career volunteering, whereas the second is an instance of casual volunteering. But, clearly, both types of volunteering are frequently needed if an event or service is be carried out effectively.

In short, casual volunteering can be absolutely crucial to a larger volunteer project or activity, even though it requires little skill, knowledge, or experience. And, as such, it can be significantly satisfying leisure for the participant. Yet this satisfaction differs profoundly from the fulfillment found in career volunteering. The latter comes from experiencing the special rewards exclusively available in all three types of serious leisure, rewards that are unavailable in casual volunteering, in particular, or in casual leisure, in general.

ENTERING VOLUNTEER WORK

Generally speaking, volunteer work offers the easiest entry of the three types of serious leisure. You need only select one of the areas listed in this chapter and contact one of the organizations or types of organizations mentioned to see if they need the sort of help you are willing and able to provide. In many instances, little advance preparation is necessary, since most organizations have specialized roles and prefer to conduct their own training when filling them.

Nonetheless, there are some important fragments of advice to add to what has already been said in this chapter. First, it seems that nearly every city of medium size or larger has some sort of central, often "computerized" clearinghouse for volunteers. It is to this organization that people may go for information on the wide range of local groups and organizations, many of them perpetually short of volunteers. The electronic revolution has made it possible to efficiently and effectively develop data banks of volunteers and match their skills with the needs of individual nonprofit organizations. These agencies usually go by the title of "volunteer center" or "voluntary action center." Moreover, most community-oriented newspapers publish a section every week or two detailing the volunteer needs at the moment of any organization in the area that contacts them. Community radio and television stations sometimes offer a similar service.

Second, some retirees may be interested in temporarily moving to another part of the country or the world to take up an attractive volunteer role. In this respect, note the number of national/international clearinghouses for volunteers that exist in both the United States and Canada. One of them, Idealist, among its several other functions, maintains an international inventory of volunteer opportunities. Volunteer Match goes one step further in striving to recruit volunteers of all ages who will provide services to seniors. Its volunteers help with transportation, yard/house cleanups, visiting/companionship, nursing home advocacy, and tax assistance. All Hands Volunteers, an organization based in the United States, provides hands-on assistance to survivors of natural disasters around the world. Similar services operate in Canada, including Charity Village (which lists volunteer opportunities by postal code and region) and the Volunteer Centre (which lists volunteer possibilities by province, as well as by opportunities at the centre).

Finally, numerous self-help volunteer data banks exist as well. Their aim is to organize specialized services for themselves as members of a particular demographic category (e.g., women, Roman Catholics, the elderly, ethnic groups). The American Association of Retired Persons (AARP) is one such organization that also offers volunteer services to certain categories of clients younger than fifty, the minimum age for AARP membership. The members of AARP supply these services.

POSITIVE SIMPLICITY IN VOLUNTEERING

The now-familiar litany of expensive-versus-inexpensive amateur and hobbyist activities applies in volunteering with much less force. Most of the time, volunteers need buy no special equipment (which is often provided by the organization), clothing, memberships, and so on. Typically, however, they are responsible for their local transportation, including commercial parking facilities when going by private car. Trips out of town may be reimbursed, including transportation, lodging, and meals. The general rule is that volunteers, though they are not paid for their services, also expect not to have to pay much for providing them. In this regard, volunteering is like most other leisure in that, in order to participate in it, we must ordinarily pay a manageable amount of money. In other words, most volunteering may be classified as more or less nonconsumptive leisure (unless local transportation costs are significant). It is, therefore, a good route for positive simplicity.

There is at least one way in which voluntary simplicity and volunteering are related that is uncommon with this attitude and either amateur or hobbyist activities. Due to its substantial altruistic motive, volunteering that is seen as directly benefiting in some way the larger community or humanity, in general, enjoys a good reputation. We usually like to see other people doing beneficial things for others. Moreover, we are inclined, where and when we can, to help them do this. In practice terms this may mean that, for example, an employer allows an employee to take off an afternoon to volunteer at a community-wide festival or other event. A spouse or other family member might assume certain domestic duties normally done by the volunteer to facilitate a similar involvement by that person.

What transforms such arrangements into instances of voluntary simplicity is that they temporarily cut back on some responsibilities (agreeable or not), enabling, in this instance, the volunteer to spend time at his or her altruistic leisure. It is important, nonetheless, to be sure that those "left holding the bag" of temporarily abandoned responsibilities do not feel exploited by the arrangement. Poisoned relationships may not be decently offset by the rewards of the session of volunteering, or be worth it under any conditions.

Chapter Six

Leisure: Casual and Project Based

We do not stop playing because we grow old.
We grow old because we stop playing.

Anonymous

In chapter 2, we discussed the types of casual and project-based leisure. The goal in this chapter is to put some flesh on these terminological bones so that retirees can find leisure of these two kinds that appeals to them. This chapter is the counterpart of the "getting started" sections of chapters 4 and 5. We turn first to the many types of casual leisure.

CASUAL LEISURE

The goal of this section is to examine each type of casual leisure in terms of its availability and usefulness for retirees. Remember that, together, these types occupy a vast territory in the world of leisure. Although I know of no research on the matter, my informal observations over the years of that world do suggest there are many, many more casual activities than those described as serious or project based. One reason for this numerical preponderance is that, unlike the other two forms, casual leisure activities may be one-shot (e.g., a bungee jump), sporadic (e.g., window shopping), or regular (e.g., suntanning on a beach every Saturday afternoon), depending on personal preferences. Thus the casual activities mentioned on the following pages should be taken as examples, a complete list being impossible to assemble at present.

Play

One common definition of play states that it is activity motivated by no other goal than the immediate pleasurable experience that flows from the activity itself. In it we are doing something, however, be it physical or mental. Examples are legion: doodling on a notepad while listening to a talk, idly bouncing a ball, whistling a simple tune, balancing an object, fiddling with something, and so on. The mental side seems to involve mostly daydreaming.

Dabbling is a special kind of play, in that it is enjoyed in some activities that are also pursued seriously. Pursued seriously, they lead to self-fulfillment and personal development. But this transition is complicated, for many a casual leisure activity holds little or no possibility of leading directly to a career in a serious pursuit. Among these are relaxation (e.g., napping, strolling in the park), sensory stimulation (e.g., sex, sightseeing, drinking alcohol), and casual volunteering (e.g., handing out leaflets on a street corner, taking tickets for a performance of an amateur play).

Furthermore, even if their casual interest is in an activity capable of being pursued seriously, some participants never take up the challenge—they never become neophytes. The stage of neophyte is the first of several in the career of any serious pursuit. However, many people, children included, prefer to do no more than dabble at tennis, bird watching, swimming, or playing the piano. Additionally, activities exist that are so complex and require so much initial skill and knowledge that entry into them, even to participate minimally, is only possible with substantial training and knowledge. Quilters, ski jumpers, sky divers, oboe players, and ballet dancers, for example, have to acquire a rudimentary level of competence before they can begin to do their activity at its simplest level. They enter their career in these pursuits as neophytes, bypassing altogether the casual leisure stage.

Relaxation

Getting a decent sense of the full variety of relaxing activities likewise defies the imagination. We saw earlier that they include idling, napping, strolling, sitting, lounging, and suntanning. That which is relaxing is, as the term implies, inactive or close to this state, as in strolling and lazily rowing a boat. Relaxation is sought as a leisure activity, however, illustrated by the foregoing list. We do these things intentionally.

Some relaxing activities are purely that, with idling, napping, and lounging or resting being prime examples. But we shall see shortly that enjoying passive entertainment and some kinds of sensory stimulation can produce the same effect. Physiologically, relaxation is the release of tension from muscles, physically lengthening the muscles, leading thereby to a state of reduced stress and anxiety.[1] Psychologically, it is the state of mind opposite that of stress and tension. Thus activities like strolling and the stretching exercises, though they demand some use of our muscles, do so in a relaxing way. Casual contemplation also fits here, exemplified in daydreaming, reminiscing, and maintaining a diary. Note, however, that contemplation can be serious when used to solve a difficult problem or reach a spiritual goal.[2]

Although this section is generally devoted to casual leisure, it is good to point out here that some serious leisure may also be relaxing at times. Moreover, its enthusiasts may welcome such a break from the effort and concentration that seriousness normally requires. On a personal note, during our canoe trips on the northern waters of Minnesota and Ontario, it seemed effortless (relaxing) paddling in leeward coves while a strong wind howled over the main lake. Wearing my other hat as a symphony orchestra bassist, the same tranquil feeling comes with a section of simple quarter or half notes when preceded by one filled with breathtaking, difficult passages. Nevertheless, such interludes are not conceived of as casual leisure, but rather as relaxed periods in serious activity that lighten the pace between the times when the music requires greater physical and mental effort.

Entertainment

In common usage one principal meaning of the verb *to entertain* is to provide the public with something enjoyable, or pleasurable, which holds their attention for the period of time the entertaining object or occasion is perceived. In entertainment that truly entertains (recognizing that some would-be entertainment flops in the perception of the individual beholder), attention is diverted from all other matters—hence the occasional usage of one of its synonyms: *diversion*. In general, these terms are employed with reference to what George Lewis called "moderately complex" (as opposed to "simple" or "highly complex") objects and occasions (e.g., a comic strip, television sitcom, popular song, Broadway play, popular novel).[3]

Of course, many things can hold our attention, among them pain, fear, serious study, and execution of a finely honed skill such as playing the violin. Yet, in the sense just set out, we would not regard these as entertaining. What is more, providing entertainment is usually not entertaining for the entertainers, since, to perform well, they must concentrate intensely. In addition to what has just been said about the nature of entertainment, it should be noted that for its consumers, when they are truly entertained, they are immersed in one kind of leisure experience. This leisure is primarily pleasurable, one of enjoyment and little else. In a nutshell, it is a type of casual leisure of its own.

In the study of casual leisure, we differentiate between *passive entertainment* (e.g., popular TV, pleasurable reading, mass-market recorded music) and *active entertainment* (e.g., games of chance, party games). One reason for this distinction is to separate those kinds of entertainment that are also relaxing from those that are not. In other words, the latter, though unskilled, still require us to pay attention to what is happening in, for example, a game of craps, bingo, roulette, or Monopoly.

How does the active form compare with its opposite number, which is the classificatory home of sedentary, "couch-potato" leisure? Here little is required for enjoyment other than turning a dial, pressing a button on a remote control, flipping a switch, attending a concert, and the like. In the passive type, an entertainment device or arrangement—a radio, television set, DVD player, or performance stage—once in action does all that is necessary to provide the sought-after diversion, as provided by one or more entertainers.

Most spectators are consumers of passive entertainment.[4] Thus, once in or at the entertainment venue (e.g., theater, concert hall, nightclub, outdoor stage), the typical member of the audience need only sit back and savor what is presented. The same may be said for attending a sports event at a court (tennis, basketball, etc.), course (e.g., golf, downhill ski, track and field), stadium, or race track, among others. And it is the same for the casual patrons of museums, art galleries, displays of public art, and so on. Finally, is not much of window shopping cut from this same hedonic cloth of passive entertainment?

By contrast, surfing Internet web pages in general must be considered active entertainment, in that it is very much an exploratory activity and requires effort beyond turning on one's computer, tablet, smartphone, or other electronic device and clicking on Google or opening up a browser. The surfer must type in search terms and then explore the sites that come up, possibly following one or more links within each. Other activities that should be regarded as active are the amusements found in the midways of fairs, exhibitions, and the like. Here the participant must be able, for instance, to throw a ball or pull a trigger while aiming at something.[5]

Pleasurable reading is active entertainment.[6] Yet what is active in reading conceived of as active entertainment? If reading were merely a matter of opening a book cover and "watching" the words inside, we could speak of it as passive entertainment. But reading for pleasure requires concentration and active attention to plot, character, storyline, and so on as fashioned by the words (something that remains constant even as many consumers turn toward e-books).[7] And there may be no visual material to aid this endeavor, as there is, for example, in entertainment television or books containing illustrational material. Flights of imagination launched from particular passages of a story are also active responses to the written material. One alternative to pleasurable reading is that which is fulfilling, a genre of literature discussed in chapter 4 in the section on the liberal arts hobbies.

Edutainment

Our discussion about entertainment as casual leisure would be incomplete if I failed to add *edutainment* to it. This idea was introduced in chapter 2 as one of the benefits of the casual form of leisure. All that need be done now is to show how entertainment sometimes goes beyond being pure hedonism, a process more complex than one might think. Thus, zoos and science museums engage in some edutainment in their displays.

In the sphere of reading, edutainment is experienced primarily through historical fiction, legends, biography/autobiography, and narrative nonfiction.[8] The challenge for readers seeking both pleasure *and* information in these four is to try to separate fact from fiction. Other readers seem content to revel in the enjoyment that such material brings—in the storyline, plot, quality of writing—and treat what they presume to be factual material as little more than interesting background to be accepted as written.

Historical fiction is, in this regard, especially beguiling. Dictionary.com defines historical fiction as a novel set either among actual events or, more broadly, in a specific period of history.[9] In this genre, information about actual events is not supposed to be fictive (or even incorrect). But how does the reader know that with certainty? Here the issue of trustworthiness takes center stage. Perhaps this is a problem to some extent for edutainment. In consuming historical fiction, readers are entertained and educated in the same breath, just as they are when they view as edutainment an exhibition in a science or history museum or watch a televised documentary. The latter normally come from an obvious authoritative source, however, whereas historical fiction is only as authoritative as its writer. This person may well be best known for the fictional side of this equation, as opposed to its factual-historical side.

Consider, as an example, Philippa Gregory's *The Other Boleyn Girl* (2002), a historical novel centered on the life of Mary Boleyn, who was a sixteenth-century aristocrat in Tudor England. This book and its five sequels (i.e., *The Queen's Fool, The Virgin's Lover*, etc.) have been alleged to contain some historical inaccuracies. Those set in the Tudor Age have been particularly challenged, with critical reviewers most upset over the fact that Gregory claimed complete accuracy. For instance, *The Other Boleyn Girl* also focuses on Henry VIII's second wife, Anne Boleyn, who is seen in the eyes of Protestants as a martyr and those of feminists as an icon. But Gregory's version of Anne's story does not entirely match the historical record.[10]

Legends are traditional stories, sometimes centered on a national hero or a folk hero, which, though based in fact, include considerable imaginary material. Since legends are collective creations, shaped and passed on over time by the people whose traditions they are, we would not ordinarily expect the same level of historical accuracy demanded of single-author historical novels. In other words, readers who consume legends as pleasurable activity typically gloss this veridical nicety; legends need only be believable, not verifiable. Still, readers of legends do acquire a sort of knowledge, even while commonly showing only limited interest in questions bearing on their accuracy and authenticity. Amazon.com lists hundreds of books under the heading of "Folktales and Legends."

Biographies and autobiographies are true stories about real people written as books or as articles gathered together in a biographic compendium (e.g., the *Who's Who* series, *The Encyclopedia of World Biography*). It is the book form that seems best suited to pleasurable reading. As a book or an article, the information conveyed is expected by readers to be as accurate as possible, peer-reviewed, and the veracity of problematic data and observations duly noted. Here casual, pleasure-oriented readers seek enjoyment in information related imaginatively and written engagingly in a narrative about a person's life. Whether this information is true matters greatly, much more so than that found in legends and historical fiction.

In other words, casual readers of biographies and autobiographies do not usually seek fulfillment in them, nor do they regard them as utilitarian literature. The facts are important, but only rarely do these readers seem inclined to check them out, challenge their accuracy, perhaps even impugn their relevance to the narrative, as would someone more analytically minded. Nevertheless, fulfillment could be, or become, a future aim of the present casual reader, as in teenage athletes who read the autobiography of a hero in their sport, coming away with an unshakable determination to excel in that activity. Initially, they probably read the book out of curiosity, expecting it to be enjoyable. Although its deeper messages were unexpected, they were presumably most welcome.

Sociable Conversation

This type of casual leisure appears to be universal. All societies seem to have places where and occasions during which members gossip, tell jokes, talk about the weather, and banter (josh, engage in repartee), among other ways to sociably converse. Telling anecdotes is another lively component of this kind of leisure. The goal in sociable conversation is to find pleasure in talking and listening to someone talk on lighthearted subjects.

Nonetheless, the line separating sociable conversation from serious talk is indistinct at times. When does joshing, for example, become ridicule and, therefore, a means of social control? When does the joke being told lampoon an outsider to the group, told with the goal of generating internal solidarity? When is the content of gossip also a form of social control aimed at particular (presumably errant) members of the group? William Harvey once made the following observation:

> There is a lust in man no charm can tame:
> Of loudly publishing his neighbor's shame:
> On eagles wings immortal scandals fly,
> while virtuous actions are born and die.[11]

The occasions on which sociable conversation occurs are, at least at present, too numerous and varied to inventory. In general, we converse sociably at work, at home, at play, and while doing errands, among many other occasions. Often such talk is mixed with serious talk. Be that as it may, sociable conversation is a vibrant kind of casual leisure in which we all engage to some extent.

Sensory Stimulation

Our senses bring us to casual leisure of great variety. Eating and drinking constitute one immense category, which lies at the very heart of the sense of taste. Another area of widespread stimulation comes with the sense of sight. It includes the vast category of sightseeing—of viewing, for example, from a vehicle or on foot the myriad natural phenomena, as well as human-made objects and structures. The popular pastime of people watching may be included here (mixed with our sense of taste when done while eating or drinking in a sidewalk café), as may the automotive and pedestrian observation of New England's colorful annual fall foliage or the grandeur of the Rocky Mountains.

Window shopping falls into the category of visual stimulation, as does a trip to the zoo or an urban overview from the likes of New York's Empire State Building or Toronto's CN Tower. Municipal parks, gardens, ponds (typically graced with some waterbirds), and fountains offer yet another category of visual casual leisure. Here and elsewhere, artistic sculptures adorn the landscape. And last, but hardly least, there is the huge variety of people and their pets that populate the streets of cities and towns. They add immensely (though not always agreeably) to our sensory experience there.

Meanwhile, the countryside provides its own smorgasbord of sensory stimulation. It runs from the sights and sounds of ranches and farmsteads to the wilder environments of rural parks and reserves. There may be wild animals to view, birds to hear and observe, and human activities to watch, as in fishing, cross-country skiing, rock climbing, and swimming.

There is also the sensory stimulation gained through sexual activity and its myriad expressions. Where two (or more) people are involved, most of the senses are commonly aroused: sight, sound, smell, touch, and possibly even taste. And since having sex is often part of a wider set of activities, probably mostly casual (e.g., dinner, movie, a stroll in the moonlight), the leisure of entertainment and sociable conversation are also enjoyed.

Casual Volunteering

We considered volunteering at length in the preceding chapter. All seventeen types covered there present a range of opportunities for people who want to serve society only or even occasionally on a casual basis. It is to be noted that, of the many casual leisure activities, only casual volunteering, like its counterpart in serious leisure, is substantially altruistic. (As with all leisure, both are also motivated by a significant degree of self-interestedness.[12]) It bears repeating here that, for all the glamour that goes with some career volunteering (e.g., serving on a board of directors, as a docent at a zoo, as a missionary in a foreign land), the value of its casual cousin is not to be underestimated. People who take tickets at the performances of the local amateur orchestra, shovel the sidewalk before winter religious services, and serve meals at community kitchens also make important unremunerated, altruistic contributions to social life.

Pleasurable Aerobic Activity

The description in chapter 2 of this kind of activity is as far as I can take it in this book. Even if pleasurable aerobic activity is as old, for example, as the children's games of tag and hide-and-seek, the scientific concept was only born in 2004. Therefore, systematic study of it is in its infancy. You are encouraged to explore your own possible activities producing this benefit. Ordinary walking (mall walking included) is as good a place to start as any. The idea is to elevate the heart rate, though not beyond the point at which the experience becomes unpleasant. Breaking a sweat might be taken as a sign that you have reached this threshold. Regularly walking faster than this leads to even better physical conditioning, of course, but it is basically another kind of activity. Depending on how it is viewed, it is either a nonwork obligation or a training regimen for a hobbyist interest like race walking or cross-country skiing.

PROJECT-BASED LEISURE

Chapter 2 contains a typology of project-based leisure, complete with examples. Thus the goal of this section is to offer some practical advice on how to get started in these projects. Remember that although a project may turn out to be reasonably long term, the intention, at least initially, is not to embark on a leisure career as an amateur or hobbyist. Rather, the orientation of the participant is to undertake something substantial and absorbing that has a clear conclusion in the foreseeable future. We look here only at one-shot projects, the occasional ones being too idiosyncratic for the goals of this section.

Making and Tinkering

Projects constructed from an interlacing, interlocking, or knot-making kit have been popular for a long time. Kits may be purchased at many of the local craft shops (in the yellow pages or online listings look under "Craft Stores," "Crafts Supplies," and "Crafts and Hobbies") or online from such outlets as Canadian Living, Hobbycraft in the United Kingdom, and Nasco in the United States.[13] Keep in mind that these establishments also sell material and books to hobbyists, whose enduring interest in the craft is typically not well served by a kit. The shops, books, and magazines for these specialized hobbyists were discussed in chapter 4.

Other Kit Assembly

Kit assembly as a leisure activity does not stop with the popular crafts discussed in the preceding paragraph. Whether as an enduring hobby or as a single project, some enthusiasts want to construct or make something else. Thus, there are outlets for categories of kits, as in the Sci Catalogue, found at the SpacecraftKits.com website, where you may purchase model kits of space-exploring machines, and Alibaba.com, which has a wide variety of woodcraft assemblies.[14] SpacecraftKits.com maintains that its kits are for "anyone with a keen interest in space exploration, almost regardless of age. The kits are not simple, and they require lots of care to assemble." Furthermore, specialty kits exist, ranging from lie detectors to chuck wagons to wooden dinosaurs (found on Google under "craft assembly kits"). For a long and miscellaneous list of such kits, see Amazon.com under the heading of "craft kits." Many of them are for children, but a retiree might want to work with a grandchild on a craft project. Amazon.com also lists a range of USS *Enterprise* model kits and model military airplane kits.

Do-It-Yourself Projects

As leisure, as opposed to nonwork obligations, handyman projects are undertaken primarily for fulfillment, some of which may even be accomplished with a modicum of skill and knowledge (e.g., build a rock wall or a fence, finish a room in the basement, plant a special garden). This could turn into an irregular series of such projects, spread out over many years, possibly even transforming the participant into a hobbyist. Projects include not only constructing or decorating something but also repairing or maintaining any complex object or system around one's home. Whether these activities are seen as leisure or as nonwork obligations depends on the participant's view of them.

On Amazon.com, you will find a long list of do-it-yourself home improvement manuals filled with projects and practical hints; most large bookstores also have home improvement sections, and some retailers (such as Lee Valley) have book departments. Some of these books are specialized, as in repair, plumbing, wiring, and things to do outside the house. The Family Handyman (familyhandyman.com) offers a wealth of projects both online and in its periodical *The Family Handyman* (twenty-two issues annually).

Liberal Arts

Genealogy

It appears that the most common approach to exploring one's family history is to create a genealogy. Typically, this is a one-shot project (not pursued as an ongoing hobby). Printed advice abounds, as a visit to Amazon will prove (under Books search using terms like "genealogy" and "family history"). The main periodicals in genealogy include *Ancestry Magazine*, *Family Tree Magazine*, *Everton's Genealogical Helper*, and *Family Chronicle*.

Related one-shot projects include the recording and possibly the scrapbooking of family events, as remembered or experienced by relatives. Both can be classified as specialized varieties of family history. The first is accomplished by analyzing, among other things, the contents of conversations (a genre of oral history), formal interviews, and letters and other written documents. The second is often carried out by rummaging through family "archives," they being any domestic storage facility (e.g., trunk, dresser, file cabinet, box in the attic). Today, personal computer files may also be valuable archival sources for this kind of material.

Additionally, local newspapers and periodicals may contain articles, obituaries, and photographs, which, when copied, should fit well in a family scrapbook. About.com's "Genealogy" website provides links to books on "journaling family memories" and "heritage scrapbooking." It also includes information about genealogical software, conferences, online courses and webinars, and educational opportunities including certification in genealogy. Obviously, at this point, the leisure project has vaulted its enthusiast into the world of devotee work, where this person may operate as a professional genealogist. Courses on family history—whether online or offered through local adult education programs—can enrich the participant's understanding of this interest as either leisure or work, as can local genealogy and family history associations and clubs.

Tourism

Tourism as project-based leisure refers to special trips and not to trips comprising part of an extensive personal tour program (a hobby). A trip to the "old country" as part of a genealogical research project is an example. Otherwise, people who are not generally enamored of foreign travel may still have a burning desire to visit a certain place or part of the world. Often, it seems that such destinations are of the old-country variety, inspired by a general curiosity about one's past rather than by a particular need to gather genealogical data. Other one-shot tours are born of a fascination with a particular part or aspect of the world, be it Paris, polar bears, or the Peruvian Andes.

Arranging for such travel is no different from arranging for tours in general. Group tours are available commercially, as provided by travel agencies or through educational noncredit courses that include a travel component (for an enticing list of the latter, search Google under "educational travel services"). Nonetheless, you may prefer to partially or wholly organize your own trips, including self-directed learning about the places you want to go and the things you want to do while there.

Renaissance Man Reading Projects

Such projects might include reading all of Shakespeare's plays, all the Pulitzer Prize winners in letters and drama for a particular year or set of years, or all novels having as their backdrop the Industrial Revolution. The resources for such projects are familiar: public libraries, bookstores (new, used, online), and friends and relatives whose copies the "Renaissance man" (a person of widespread talent and learning) may borrow. Book clubs, whether interaction is online or face-to-face, are rarely this specialized. Moreover, the social potential of this pastime is limited, for few of the reader's associates will have so deep an interest in it.

Activity Participation

As with the Renaissance man reading projects and the one-shot tours, some participant activities lend themselves to a singular experience. They appear to be mainly of the nature-challenge type—namely, a long canoe or backpacking trip; a one-off, nontechnical mountain ascent (most famously Fuji and Kilimanjaro); a balloon tour; a parachute jump (sometimes receiving the needed instruction the same day); or a cave tour. A list of cave tours exists on the Real Adventures website.[15] Most large North American cities have companies offering one-shot parachute jumps.

Volunteering

Many of the previously mentioned seventeen types of volunteering can be pursued as one-shot projects. Commonly, there is a public call for volunteers made in the mass media, online using lists of diverse kinds, and in notices posted in public places. Alternatively, an e-mail message or telephone inquiry to the headquarters of the volunteer group of interest should result in information about its needs for help.

We lack hard data on the proportion of all volunteering that is, in fact, of the one-shot kind. But we may confidently say that a sizable demand exists for it. Conferences of all sorts rely heavily on volunteer help, as do sporting competitions, arts festivals, and special exhibitions mounted in zoos, museums, and science centers. The vast majority of people who volunteer to help restore communities or wildlife following a natural or human-made disaster are seeking project-based leisure. The disaster might be a hurricane, earthquake, oil spill, or industrial accident.

Arts Projects

Entertainment Theater

Included under this heading are skits, one-shot community pageants, and nonprofessional films and videos. Sets of photos and slides are also instances of artistic project-based leisure.

Search under "skits" on Amazon.com for miscellaneous books on the subject, some of which are written for children or adolescents. Also try Skits Galore! and the skits offered by iComedyTV [16] as well as the plethora of sites that come up after searching Google for "skits." Many of these sites present enough information about their skits for most people to mount them without further consultation.

The *American Heritage Dictionary* defines a "pageant" as follows:

1. An elaborate public dramatic presentation that usually depicts a historical or traditional event.
2. A spectacular procession or celebration.
3. Colorful showy display; pageantry or pomp. [17]

Creating and presenting a pageant is clearly a group affair. Furthermore, its content will be determined substantially by the kind of event to be presented in pageant form, as well as the imagination of its architects. A search on Google reveals that most of what is available there—and it is available in great variety and profusion—are sites concerned with beauty pageants. The books listed under "pageant" on Amazon.com, when they meet our definition, center primarily on Christmas pageants and those organized to parade human beauty. *Pageant Magazine* and *Pageant Girl* offer regular news and advice on beauty contests in the United States and the United Kingdom, respectively.

Home films, videos, and slide shows have become ever easier to carry off, thanks to user-friendly equipment including the rise of digital cameras with the ability to produce images on a par with professional photography, television, and film production. The same may be said for displays of photos, which these days are commonly presented on a television screen as slides—most DVD and Blu-ray players allow display of photographs saved on removable media such as DVD-ROMs and memory cards. The technical know-how needed for these projects is found in a wide selection of computer software programs, with the photos and videos themselves being captured using a camera, iPod, cellphone, or similar device. Look for discussions of the artistic side of these productions in various books, many of which are listed on Amazon.com (search using "home video production"). A number of magazines and websites are also available, although they are better suited to the hobbyist than the one-shot project enthusiast.

Public Speaking

Preparing a talk for a reunion, an after-dinner speech, an oral position statement on an issue to be discussed at a community meeting, and so on number among the many occasions when you might need to give a public presentation. There are books galore on this subject (see Amazon.com under "public speaking"). If you are interested in making a hobby of this art, you might want to join a local chapter of Toastmasters or some other speakers' club. Still, the present subject is the leisure project of a single occasion, an imminent date with the rostrum that the person looks forward to but still must prepare for.[18] Books and certain online sites are the best instructional resource for this kind of undertaking. Toastmasters International also offers a multitude of hints.[19] In searching Google using the term "public speaking," you will note that most of the entries cater to professionals in this field. Nevertheless, there is also the occasional article aimed at the nonprofessional. It will help those for whom public speaking is a one-shot project.

Memoirs

Found under this heading are audio, visual, and written productions by the elderly; life histories and autobiographies (all ages); and accounts of personal events (all ages). This is often of interest specifically to retirees, many of whom are elderly, but, even comparatively young ones at around age fifty-five have had a wealth of experiences. Moreover, some of them would like to describe and evaluate these experiences in some public way.[20] Additionally, in our fast-paced, ever-changing modern world, as people live into their eighties and nineties, their past increasingly contrasts with the present in which they and their much-younger friends and relatives now live. Some seniors are inclined to talk about this disjuncture using such terminology as "in the (good) old days," "when I was your age," "I can remember when we didn't have . . . ," or similar lead-ins to a bout of reminiscences. Some younger listeners find these observations interesting, if not edifying, whereas others care little about the past thus revealed.

Seniors face a dilemma when they want to converse this way while sensing that their observations on a bygone era may be unwelcome. On the one hand, they might remain silent on such matters, stifling their impulse to contextualize the conversation in what they consider an enlightening way that simultaneously enables them to briefly enjoy the limelight. On the other hand, they might introduce a comparison like those described above, while risking its rejection by the others in the exchange. A way around this dilemma for seniors is to suppress most of their spontaneous reminiscences and instead write out as a personal memoir in the form of prose or poetry those aspects of their past that they want to share with whoever would read what they have written.

In principle such a memoir could be written, audio, or visual, as in an essay, piece of poetry, recorded oral statement, or videotaped account. In practice, it is probable that most memoirs are of the essay variety, but oral and visual types are becoming ever more common given advances in and proliferation of facilitative recording equipment. Poetry would seem to be the least popular medium for these memoirs, although seniors have been observed to warm to this way of telling about their past.[21]

Social World

Many leisure projects are pursued within a fairly limited social world, wherein the participant is linked to very few other people, if any at all. Mostly this person operates alone in the making of or tinkering with something or in the reading of books or magazines. In such projects contact with others may be required to obtain necessary supplies or services, and one or more admirers may turn up to check out the completed endeavor. Yet the core activity in these kinds of making and tinkering is typically enjoyed in isolation.

In comparison, other leisure projects offer a richer social world. The arts projects, for instance, are inherently social, since they are prepared for an audience and require a place where these artists can present them. Even writing a memoir presumes that someone will read, view, or listen to what the author has created. It is the same with most volunteering and virtually all touring projects. True, some floral, faunal, and environmental volunteering projects, for example, can be conducted alone (e.g., nursing a wounded bird back to health, cleaning up a littered section of a highway), but most volunteering directly serves other people. Indeed, most volunteering is conducted through some sort of formal organization or established informal group, thereby enriching still further the volunteer's social world.

The need for advice on or instruction in preparing the project adds yet another element to its social world. We have seen in this regard the importance of books, magazines, websites, specialized shops, and clubs and larger organizations. Finally, other people may be needed to facilitate the project, often of the service variety. Thus, a pilot and plane must be located for the parachute project, a tour company for the touring project, and a guide for the caving experience. If the project includes as preparation taking a course or two, then instructors enter the social world of the project participant.

In short, there is in project-based leisure as a category of activities something for both the reclusive and the gregarious. Nevertheless, if a sense of being deeply involved with others is a main goal, then the richest social worlds will be found in some of the casual and serious leisure activities. And many of those in serious leisure offer such involvement over a period of many years, if not decades.

Positive Simplicity in Leisure Projects

The cost of project-based leisure runs the gamut from virtually free to enormously expensive. Putting on a skit may consume a lot of time, but it can be monetarily cost free. By contrast, signing up for one of the proposed trips into space offered by Virgin Galactic starts at $200,000. Generally speaking, volunteering and the arts projects generate plenty of leisure for relatively little cost. The same holds for reading projects, especially if the books in question are borrowed. However, in making and tinkering the costs rise, sometimes substantially, with the price of kits, materials, instruction, and so forth. And tourism and activity participation normally require significant expenditures. But the family history projects are generally within the budget of many people, although they are rarely completely free of expenses. Even a scrapbook costs something.

When it comes to positive simplicity, project-based leisure has a special place. For one thing, projects are limited in time; the participant does not see a long career here. Therefore, a relatively high financial cost for one of them will, at least, not be a continual expense, as is true for certain serious and casual pursuits. Two, although we will discuss this in more detail in the next chapter, leisure projects can act as attractive and affordable fillers between intense periods of work and serious leisure. They can also make for exciting free-time alternatives in a life otherwise filled with casual leisure. Three, taking up the occasional leisure project helps retirees fine-tune their set of leisure activities. As they settle into their leisure lifestyle in retirement, they learn about how much time they want to devote to each activity. Where there are gaps, they may want to take up a project with which to fill them.

CONCLUSION

For the World Health Organization (WHO), the goal of "successful" aging is reached through the process of "active aging."[22] Their recommendation to the burgeoning aging population of the world is that its members remain active by continuing to make positive contributions to citizenship, society, and the economy. Moreover, they should do this while maintaining responsibility for their personal well-being in later life.

In the language of this book, active aging will take place primarily in leisure (including devotee work). Nevertheless, WHO's recommendation is easier for the young-old to honor than for the old-old (people aged seventy-five to eighty-five years and beyond). The latter typically have less stamina, poorer memories, various disabilities, and other impediments that are bound to limit their capacity to contribute to the community and be responsible for their well-being.

That said, project-based leisure can help. Much of it is short-term and possible to carry off with limited preparation. Some of it is amenable to a sedentary lifestyle. This is ideal stuff for the old-old, whose sense of well-being can be elevated through such activity.

As for casual leisure among retirees of all ages, it might seem to be too trivial to justify any attention in this book, other than a passing glance. It is, after all, pure hedonism. Nonetheless, as we saw in chapter 2, hedonism and its activities conceived of as casual leisure have their benefits. They also have their place in the retiree's leisure lifestyle. As for the leisure projects, I have already briefly noted their role as fillers in that leisure lifestyle. But there is more to it than that.

Chapter Seven

Planning a Leisure Lifestyle

The busier we are, the more leisure we have.

William Hazlitt

William Hazlitt, nineteenth-century English writer and painter, has written a formula for a captivating leisure lifestyle. Framed in the language of this chapter, the advice is to develop a rich leisure lifestyle, one full to the brim of the most satisfying and rewarding activities you can arrange to pursue. Retirement, unless narrowed by the need to work part-time, is the stage of life during which this lifestyle can reach its greatest efflorescence. Now leisure may be sought full-time, which is often done in some combination of two, if not all three, of the serious, casual, and project-based forms. Alternatively, some people pursue their leisure in parallel with part-time devotee work. Yet, given that an attractive leisure lifestyle has enormous appeal, selfishness can take root. It is a weed quite capable of choking out the positiveness of life in retirement.

This scenario suggests a need for careful planning. A rich leisure lifestyle does not magically appear. Rather, retirees who want one should consciously work up a set of attractive, feasible activities (many of them discussed earlier), then choose among them and, finally, blend those chosen into an appealing lifestyle.

We look first at the idea of lifestyle and next at the several types of leisure lifestyle. Lifestyles, which always have a geographic basis, are nonetheless framed in time and social relations. The prickly question of leisure selfishness is covered in the conclusion.

NATURE OF THE LEISURE LIFESTYLE

Michael Sobel defined lifestyle as "a distinctive, hence recognizable, mode of living."[1] According to this definition, lifestyle consists not of the values, attitudes, and orientations of the person, but of the routine, tangible patterns of behavior that are "eminently observable or deducible from observation." For our purposes, those patterns of behavior are evident in what people routinely think and do while pursuing their leisure activities. More particularly, a leisure lifestyle is primarily made up of the lifestyles associated with each leisure activity in the participant's set of such activities.

Serious leisure seems more likely to generate complex patterns of behavior than its counterpart, casual leisure. An exciting, complex lifestyle awaits the person who routinely pursues a serious leisure career in, say, amateur theater, volunteer work with the mentally handicapped, the hobby of model railroading, or the pursuit of mountain climbing. And perhaps the leisure enthusiast will also discover exciting, if not less complex, lifestyles in such casual-leisure interests as hot-tubbing and weekend beer parties. But other forms of casual leisure—for example, routine suntanning or strolling in the park—are often not shared with others. Therefore, they contribute to a lifestyle that is, in part, reclusive and, for that reason alone, also simpler.

TYPES OF LIFESTYLES IN RETIREMENT

What people like to do in their leisure depends in significant part on how much they like to be on the move. Here "on the move" means temporarily leaving home (their dwelling) and immediate neighborhood for a more distant place, this happening in the name of leisure. In principle, being on the move is especially germane for those retirees who like this lifestyle, and who now have more time for it than at any other period in their lives. And, for those who like being on the move, just how far and how often they care to go to a distant place are major questions. Meanwhile, other retirees—many in the old-old category or in the unpleasant situation in which being on the move is either physically or psychologically awkward—avoid as much as possible leaving home and neighborhood. Broadly put, lifestyle always has a geographic basis, even if that basis is not the same for everyone.

The leisure lifestyles of most retirees conform reasonably well to one or two of the five geographic types described below. Pick out the type you fit, or are striving to fit, and then compare yourself with friends and relatives by trying to identify their type. These comparisons will help you see, in real-life terms, others' lifestyles, ones that you might conceivably adopt. Or, if you find them unattractive, you should explain to yourself why you prefer your own over those of the others. Such an exercise enhances lifestyle planning.

Homebody Lifestyle

Homebodies are, for leisure purposes, normally not on the move. Granted, they must occasionally, though usually only briefly, leave home and immediate neighborhood to meet such nonwork obligations as buying groceries and seeking medical help. They may also have to go out for more pleasant reasons such as to obtain equipment, supplies, services, and the like needed for their domestic leisure. Further, they might occasionally break with this lifestyle by enjoying the odd ride in the countryside or a trip to a distant city, say, to visit a friend or relative. In other words, for the homebodies, their most important leisure activities are found where they live, even while sporadic obligations and leisure interests push them beyond its walls.

Yet, in general, homebodies find that their domestic leisure is sufficiently attractive and that, consequently, the other leisure lifestyles hold little interest. Nevertheless, for retirees forced to remain at home as dictated by a physical or mental disability, home and its available leisure may make it as much a refuge as a retreat. For them leisure at home is appealing, in part because it spares them the discomforts often encountered when they must venture into the wider community.

Leisure homebodies are a diverse lot. Whatever their age, some people are simply much inclined toward the leisure available at home. Others find it attractive—it *is* leisure—but have had their choices narrowed by special circumstances. One may be low income. The old-old are another such group, who may be homebodies in their own dwelling or in a residence. People with mental or physical disabilities may, as previously noted, find that their condition leaves them little choice but to function as a leisure homebody. And part-time devotee workers whose jobs take them away from home may be disposed to spending the remaining hours of the day or week immersed in some sort of domestic bliss. Lastly, recluses seem driven to stay home, cocooned in seclusion. This they do, it seems, not so much to avail themselves of the leisure inside as to escape the threats perceived to exist outside.

Homebody Leisure

Nowadays, the Internet is arguably most effectively and enjoyably explored when at home. More particularly, computer and video-console games may be played while nestled in the comforts of home, even as "massively multiplayer online role-playing games" (MMORPGs) bring the homebound player into contact with thousands of other players linked together online, as do an increasing number of console games that incorporate online interaction. Additionally, the Internet and a couple of computers enable serious sports buffs to follow simultaneously several broadcast games. This arrangement is best carried out at home, whether one's own or that of someone else. That said, video-gaming today need no longer be confined to home or other stationary locations. Tablets and handheld gaming systems enable people to carry on some of these activities wherever Wi-Fi is available.

All the other games mentioned in chapter 4 are also commonly played at home, many of them involving two or more others (even crosswords, acrostic puzzles, and brain teasers can become social, as when the player asks someone else for advice on a word or a solution). Thus homebodies are not always or even necessarily reclusive, in that friends or relatives, if not both, may come around regularly or sporadically to enrich the leisure of the former. This may happen not only for games but also for such sports as croquet, horseshoes, pool/billiards, darts, and table tennis. Moreover, collective leisure in the form of chamber music, barbershop quartet singing, jazz jam sessions, and even pickup basketball or hockey games (given the space and necessary installations) are also possible homebody activities.

Turning to the individual arts, those of painting, writing, sculpting, craftwork, and others are well-established homebody activities. The same is true for collecting and making and tinkering. And the liberal arts hobbies, based as they are on reading, are mostly pursued in one's own abode.[2]

Even some kinds of volunteering can be carried out at home. Known as, among other terms, "e-volunteering" and "virtual volunteering," participants here use information and communications technology to enable and facilitate volunteering at a distance from their group or organizational base.[3] E-volunteering can take the form of serious, casual, or project-based leisure.

And, speaking of casual leisure, the domestic scene offers an immense variety. Here you may relax, have sociable conversations, and enjoy all sorts of entertainment running from television to videos, CDs, and solitary card games. You may also find sensory stimulation as diverse as sex, potted plants, casually read periodicals, decorative wall hangings, recorded music, animal movements, and the like. Home also appears to be the most common location for pleasurable aerobic activity, mostly accomplished using certain video programs. As for play, how many people dabble at home on a guitar, keyboard, banjo, or recorder? At-home dabblers may play at writing poetry, singing tunes, sketching still lives, and molding clay, to mention just a few options. Then there is the mountain of opportunities for sociable conversation made possible on Facebook, Twitter, YouTube, Blogger, and other social media.

It is evident that homebody leisure can be a main arena for positive simplicity. Here, at least, costs of room and board are minimized, while those of transportation may be so low as to vanish (being able to walk to acquire necessities). Of course, one might spend a small fortune on a home sound system, food and medical care for pets, or hobby-related computer software. Collecting objects, as observed earlier, can be notoriously expensive, as seen in the acquisition of coins, guns, paintings, and musical instruments. Some homebodies, however, may only be able to pursue these expensive hobbies because they have economized substantially by doing much of their leisure at home.

Traveler Lifestyle

This is the free-time passion of the inveterate tourist. And being on the move to new destinations and old ones worth revisiting is this person's leisure raison d'être. Most of these tourists must also spend some time at home, during which they recover financially, prepare for the next voyage, and engage in some of the homebody, townie, and outbacker leisure activities discussed in this chapter. And, for the traveler type, the trips are reasonably frequent, perhaps three or four a year. One exception to this pattern is the "RVing" seniors, a number of whom live full-time in their house trailers. These they drive across North America from one camping site or trailer park to another.[4]

Some travelers organize their tours according to a liberal arts interest. They are, for example, enamored of history or architecture, frequently augmenting their reading in such specialties with travel to representative regional, national, or worldwide sites. These travelers constitute one of several combined types of leisure lifestyle, in this instance the homebody-travelers. Their strategy is to stay home for a spell, where they read about their destinations, save up money for travel, and plan the next trip.

Other travelers on the move are propelled by a desire to view celebrated scenery and related flora and fauna. They are essentially casual leisure sightseers. For instance, they are keen on seeing the Alps, the Galapagos Islands, the seascape of Fiji, or the wildlife and physical environment of the Antarctic. As just mentioned, sightseers are inclined to do some reading in advance of their trips. But it is typically of the preparatory kind, rather than being fulfilling liberal arts material. That is, sightseers are not commonly interested in, let us say, a profound (liberal arts) knowledge of the history, biology, and politics of the Galapagos. This would ordinarily take some years to acquire. Sightseeing brings a feast primarily for the eyes, though the ears or nose might be stimulated as well (e.g., hearing the barking of sea lions, smelling the sulphur of a hot springs). It is not, however, supposed to provide an intellectual feast.

A related type of sightseer is the cultural traveler. One difference is that this type commonly wants to experience the local cultures of cuisine, marketplace, museums, and street scenes, to mention a few of the attractions. Scenic vistas are included where possible and time and money permit. Most cultural travelers are casual leisure participants. They most commonly participate by joining a commercial tour, as provided by travel agencies and tour companies. The travel-study programs offer a more profound knowledge base for the culture to be studied, turning the tour into a leisure project.

Some devotee work, as carried out part-time during semi-retirement, has a traveling component, albeit not ordinarily a touristic one. Consultants may travel often to meet with their clients. Semi-retired professional performing artists usually cut back on the amount of traveling they did when employed full-time, but this reduction is only partial. As a third example, consider the town planner who, even as a part-time employee, must travel occasionally to distant communities to advise on, say, public transportation routes or the layout of a new suburb.

Of the five types of leisure lifestyles commonly experienced by retirees, the traveler generally faces the thinnest opportunity for practicing positive simplicity. A significant part of the problem is that tourist travel is costly, be it by sea, land, or air. True, cycling, staying in hostels, and preparing one's own meals do cut costs significantly. But for many retirees such spartan living has lost its appeal, if indeed it ever had any. The comforts of home call loudly when flexibility wanes, bones protrude, fatigue easily sets in, and other accompaniments of aging reduce resiliency. These comforts may be found on many trips, but only at considerable expense.

Additionally, suitable clothing may constitute a major expense. A Southern Californian contemplating a trip to the Antarctic, for instance, will need a wardrobe very different from and likely more expensive than the one at home. People living in dry climates, when visiting places like Scotland and India (especially in monsoon season), may want to stock up on rain wear. Travelers interested in trips involving substantial amounts of walking or hiking will wisely buy and maintain appropriate footwear.

The positive nature of these expenses is evident; they do enhance the leisure experience. Here, scrimping on such purchases may land the buyer with poor-quality goods and a spoiled tour. Here the rule of thumb, à la positive simplicity, is to find the best product at the cheapest price. One way to accomplish this is to patronize an outdoor equipment cooperative, where sales personnel often know through experience the strengths and weaknesses of the products they sell.[5] More generally, consider reading Rolf Magener's *Trip Tips: Travel Tips for the Independent Traveler* (2012), which is available in paperback and Kindle editions.

Townie Lifestyle

The townie likes being on the move *within* the local community. A main avenue for this is the plethora of opportunities in career, casual, or project-based volunteering, or in a combination of these. The eighteen sectors discussed in chapter 5 show, for the larger cities, how widespread and varied these opportunities can be, as well as the extent to which a retiree may become immersed in communal activities. As a category of townie leisure, volunteering offers by far the greatest range of potential community contacts.

The collective amateur and hobbyist activities, though numerous, are, when compared with the communal volunteering opportunities, smaller in number. Nevertheless, the rehearsals and performances of the larger dance, musical, choral, and theatrical groups must, of necessity, be held in places designed for such activity. This requirement rules out their members' homes. Many of these groups meet weekly (community-theater rehearsals may, however, be scheduled as often as thrice weekly). Performances, depending on the art, run from one or two days to as many as ten, with four productions per season being common.

Amateur science, as we shall see shortly, is, by and large, an outbacker activity (the definition of "outbacker" is given in the next section). Nonetheless, there is at times a home component, too. Some astronomers view the heavens through backyard telescopes. Laboratory work in amateur botany, entomology, and mineralogy, for example, is commonly carried out at home. By contrast, amateur history often nudges its enthusiasts into the community and its specialized libraries, bookstores, and archives. Local historians may also need to leave home to interview (usually) elderly individuals whose past is of historical interest.

Collective amateur sport, individual and group entertainment, and the body-centered hobbies (except for home-based body building) lead to an essentially townie lifestyle. In sport, players must for their practices and games head for the town's parks, gyms, fields, arenas, and so on. The equivalents for the entertainers are the local parks (in good weather), nightclubs, community centers, church basements, and concert halls, among others. Among the body-centered activities gymnasts also head for the gyms, whereas ballroom dancers take to the studios and nightclubs equipped with dance floors. Elsewhere, the roller skaters, ice skaters, and swimmers workout in their own distinctive town facilities, sometimes located at some distance from where these participants live.

The collecting, making, and tinkering hobbies, which are commonly pursued at home, are nonetheless sometimes organized in clubs. As a result, members must occasionally leave home to attend meetings and participate in other club activities. These organizations tend to be the ones that promote such community-wide events as hobbyist demonstrations (e.g., model railroad displays, quilt shows, doll collections), sales (e.g., baked and canned goods, knitted wear, craft products), and concerts (e.g., folk music, barbershop singing). Be that as it may, the core activities of the home-based hobbies are pursued domestically, which helps justify placing their participants in the homebody lifestyle.

A main part—possibly the only part—of the casual leisure side of the townie lifestyle revolves around particular third places. Ray Oldenburg has named these the "great good places."[6] For leisure, people hang out at a certain club, pub/bar, coffee shop, bookstore, café, or branch of the public library. Other such hangouts include certain parks, hair salons, street corners, and shopping centers. Wherever they meet, participants enjoy the ambiance and sometimes a conversation with other people. If available, they may also prize the food and drink, the ongoing leisure activities (mostly games), the reading material, and the television programming. In England, "quiz evenings" (a knowledge game) are popular pub activities for younger men and women.[7] As for the conversational aspect of hanging out at the "great good places," note that it is possible to frequent nearly all of them without talking to anyone, except possibly only enough to ask for something.

Otherwise, casual leisure as play, relaxation, entertainment, sensory stimulation, and pleasurable aerobic activity seems to be enjoyed primarily at home. Typically, there are sporadic sorties to community sites to partake of one or more of these activities, but most of the time participants do them where they live. This pattern, however, does not necessarily signal the presence of a homebody leisure lifestyle. In harmony with what was just said, retirees leading a townie lifestyle have serious leisure and project-based activities that justify classifying them thus. Those who do hang out regularly at one or more great good places are, therefore, best classified as having a homebody/townie leisure lifestyle. Nevertheless, as retirees age, the amount of leisure sought outside their home declines. The homebody/townie lifestyle eventually gives way to an ever more unadulterated homebody existence.

Part-time devotee workers, unless they engage in their serious pursuit from home, lead a townie leisure lifestyle. Working outside the home keeps them involved in one or more spheres of community life, as these spheres are linked to the job. With less time for other leisure than full-time retirees, these workers may, nonetheless, want to fill out their typical week with some of the many activities discussed in this book. As with all retirees, the challenge is to craft the most interesting and exciting leisure lifestyle possible, given the temporal, monetary, and interpersonal constraints that we all must deal with.

Outbacker Lifestyle

This lifestyle is the one experienced by retirees who try to spend a good part of most weeks of the year outside their community of residence in certain rural areas within approximately a day's drive from it. "Rural" refers to such parts of the countryside as farms, ranches, nonurban parks, wilderness areas, game preserves, and the like. That outbackers *try* to spend some time each week in the outback refers to the fact they may be stymied in attempting to do so. They may be (usually) temporarily denied this kind of leisure by such constraints as weather, natural disasters (e.g., flooding, forest fires), and environmental protection directives (e.g., closures to protect animals, control erosion, prevent overfishing).

The outbacker's leisure lifestyle typically consists of several rural outdoor activities pursued only during certain seasons of the year. In principle, the activities may be either serious or casual leisure, though most probably the typical ensemble is comprised of some of both. Furthermore, the outbacker may want to become involved in a few leisure projects—for example, cleaning up a trout stream, reconstructing a hiking or cycling trail, or eradicating an invasive species.

Nearly all the serious outdoor activities done in the outback are hobbies, with the amateur sciences of astronomy, ornithology, mineralogy, entomology, and botany being the main exceptions. All these pursuits have been studied under the rubric of "nature challenge activities," a reasonably complete list of which appears in the appendix.[8] Nature presents physical challenges in all its elements: air, water, land, flora and fauna, and snow and ice. Some of these challenges are also available in towns and cities (e.g., bird watching, entomological research, skating, rowing), but the outbacker often prefers much more sparsely inhabited conditions, if not those completely uninhabited.

Since most outbackers live in towns and cities, getting to and from their areas of interest in the outback is frequently time-consuming. Thus, part of their leisure lifestyle is routine travel to these places, which, for committed full-time retirees, may occur as much as two or three times a week. Furthermore, since many outdoor activities are seasonal, so are the patterns of travel. For instance, participants usually have to travel farther to find downhill skiing in winter than to watch birds in any season, to find trail hiking (spring, summer, fall) than to photograph flowers (primarily summer).

Clearly, inveterate outbackers pursue a number of serious leisure outdoor activities, such that they have something to do of this nature throughout the year. For example, one might fish in spring, summer, and fall and in fall hunt birds or animals as well. Winter could be a season for snowmobiling. My personal outback activities are mountain hiking in spring, summer, and fall, then turning to cross-country skiing and snowshoeing in winter. Some of our party mix the hiking with floral photography in summer.

These are but a sample. If you are interested in principle in the serious leisure side of the outbacker lifestyle, you might want to create from the appendix your own four-season package of activities. What you can do depends on which activities are financially accessible and routinely available nearby. The outbacker lifestyle certainly includes, after a day's drive, staying overnight for one or more days to participate in a given activity. It also includes, when winter closes down the courses at home, heading for a warm climate for three months of full-time golfing.

Positive Simplicity

Outback activities span nearly the full range of costs. Downhill skiing approaches the top of this scale, mainly because of the fees the ski resorts demand. Most of the activities done in the air, with the exception of snowkiting (surfing, boarding), are also in the high-price league. So it is as well for the water-based activities, though surfing, free diving, and water-skiing/wakeboarding (pulled with someone else's boat) are only moderately expensive. One need simply buy a board or skis if they can't be routinely borrowed. Land is the home of the largest number of affordable activities. The last three in that classification in the appendix are, however, by far the costliest in that group. The floral and faunal activities are generally relatively inexpensive, especially after the initial purchase of a decent telescope, microscope, or camera, or of fishing and hunting gear. Leisure in ice or snow is relatively inexpensive, the purchase and maintenance of a snowmobile being a major exception, along with, of course, those fees at the ski resorts.

Casual Leisure in the Outback

Serious leisure outbackers probably constitute a minority of all the people who find leisure in such regions (no scientific data exists on this ratio). The outback, in its more reachable aspects, is immensely popular for picnicking, strolling, sightseeing, and camping (on sites easily reached by road). Many people also go there to casually cycle, boat, fish, sled, swim, ride (rented) horses, or collect natural objects. Berry picking is popular where the outback has produced a sufficient and accessible supply of plants.

Play in the outback sometimes occurs as exploration in nature, manifested in a casual stroll off-trail in the forest, along a beach, or through the desert. The goal of these sorties is simple: "to see what one can see." To be sure, this can be a treacherous pastime for people unaware of the dangerous habits of the local beasts (insects and reptiles included) and, in forests, for those who, failing to attend to their whereabouts, become lost. There is also in some forests the threat of poisonous plants, with poison ivy, being found throughout much of North America, arguably the most infamous.

Part-Time Retirement Lifestyle

This is the leisure lifestyle of retirement-age workers whose work activities are not fired by occupational devotion. The occupational devotee is, when at work, essentially pursuing a kind of serious leisure. Not so with the nondevotee worker, who is attached to the job for other reasons.

That is, many part-time workers/retirees continue employment because they need the money it produces. Some continue thus because they would miss their colleagues should they break with them through full-time retirement. Maybe they would miss the money, as well. Some continue because they have all the leisure they want in part-time retirement. Whatever the reason, part-time retirement/employment is seen as a sensible arrangement for those living this lifestyle.

Leisure in part-time retirement may be pursued in any of the other four lifestyles, albeit inevitably outside the oftentimes rigid temporal demands of the part-time job. For instance, working Monday through Wednesday allows a four-day leisure window, compared with a Monday-Wednesday-Friday work schedule. The latter allows only one block of free time, and it lasts only two days. That nonwork obligations must be fitted into the four days of weekly free time further truncates the manipulability for leisure purposes of those discretionary hours. Such obligations can be substantial in old age, what with needs for routine special exercise, say, to recover from a hip replacement, or routine medical procedures, as required by recent cataract or prostate surgery.

The homebody lifestyle offers, on the whole, the greatest flexibility, a highly practical feature when weekly free time is markedly reduced. True, there may be schedules to respect here, such as those required in e-volunteering and in following simultaneously a slate of broadcast sports games. Nevertheless, this lifestyle minimizes the time lost in commuting, normally a nonrewarding, but necessary period of time between rewarding stints of leisure (and work). Meanwhile, nonrewarding commuter time looms as an unwanted necessity in all the other leisure lifestyles.[9] The part-time worker/retiree, as with the part-time devotee worker/retiree, is automatically involved in one or more spheres of community life, mostly as these spheres are linked to the job. The desire for more of such involvement as leisure may, therefore, be weakened, rendering the townie lifestyle somewhat less attractive. Leisure projects may also be especially attractive for the part-time retiree, whether carried out at home or in the community.

TEMPORAL FRAMES OF RETIREMENT LEISURE

The dominant issue here is when and according to what schedule, if any, do retirees pursue their leisure. In planning for a leisure lifestyle in retirement, it is important to consider the daily, weekly, monthly, and seasonal temporal frames of the activities that might be adopted. The activities might be appealing, whereas their scheduling requirements could be much less so.

Daily Frame

The daily requirements are those that arise almost every day or on certain days of the week. I use the phrase "almost every day" to refer to activities that, perhaps ideally, should be enacted daily but, in practice, can occasionally be skipped for one day. Slacking off in this way, participants can still maintain and advance their expertise in a serious pursuit. Such a requirement is critical to every skill-based activity, from playing musical instruments to training in sports. Finding the greatest rewards here means adhering to an almost-every-day schedule of practicing or working out in the basic and advanced techniques. In some other activities, however, improvement in skill comes with actually doing the core activity, exemplified in knitting, woodworking, and craftwork. Participants in these hobbies do not ordinarily practice or work out. Rather, they get better at their hobby by making new wooden, knitted, or crafted objects.

Normally, participants have some degree of choice as to when during the day they engage in their hobbies. One of the attractions of leisure in general is that participants have, more than in the other two domains of life, considerable discretion as to how they deploy the minutes and hours of each day. In particular, they may decide it is best for them to workout in the morning, knit in the evening, or practice the piano in the afternoon. They may further decide how much time to devote to each. Note, too, that some almost-every-day leisure is found away from home, in such establishments as commercial gyms and certain "great good places." Their hours of business must be taken into account. In the end, part of the appeal of leisure is being able to set your own pace and develop an optimal leisure lifestyle around the different temporal requirements of your activities.

Weekly Frame

In much of home-based leisure, the day-to-day routine spreads across the weeks, a pattern that may, however, have to be adapted to the weekly requirements of leisure pursued outside the home. For example, some retirees belong to organizations that convene weekly in the evenings or on the weekends. Such schedules are popular, since they accommodate the work obligations of the non-retirees in the group, who usually constitute the majority of members. The collective arts groups commonly rehearse at night, and many sports teams also practice at this time (or early in the morning). For these same reasons, many adult education courses are offered on Saturday or at night, once or twice a week.

In contrast, many of the clubs and informal groups devoted to activities in the outback are active on weekends, unless composed exclusively of seniors. The latter have the advantage of being able to frequent the outback during the week, when they have less human and vehicular traffic to contend with. The distances to be covered in reaching the outback are typically such that the better part of a given day is usually consumed in a single session of leisure. One reason for the lure of weekends and statutory holidays is obvious here. Moreover, as observed earlier, carefully planned schedules for outback activities can be undermined by the weather and official closures.

Clubs and informal groups established to enable gaming and certain participatory activities are also likely to meet weekly. This is a preferred occasion for pursuing the leisure in question. Groups interested in chess, role-playing games, and certain card games (e.g., poker, bridge) attest to this pattern. It is the same with clubs devoted to orienteering and geocaching.

Monthly Frame

Most of the monthly requirements emanate from clubs and other organizations that meet with this frequency (some meet semimonthly). Taken alone, these gatherings constitute for retirees but a small proportion of all their leisure activities. Social clubs—their main attractions are a lunch or dinner and sociable conversation—tend to operate according to a monthly schedule. Science clubs usually hold monthly meetings, at which there is typically a guest speaker and, invariably, plenty of shoptalk about doing the focal science. Hobbyist clubs of collectors and makers and tinkers also tend to follow this pattern of monthly meetings. Interestingly, the pattern persists, despite the parallel proliferation of online discussion groups that allow conversation and interaction at any time.

The scientific and hobbyist organizations facilitate certain amateur and hobbyist pursuits, whereas the core activities of those pursuits are carried out elsewhere. In contrast, similar to the enabling groups discussed above, some clubs and informal groups that meet weekly actually enable their core activities. In effect, members of the latter have no desire to wait a month to engage in their passion. A week is often too long as it is.

Some community events are also held monthly. For instance, a cinema may show a particular genre of film on such a schedule; buffs will be sure to attend. Certain bars and restaurants are known for offering a featured monthly drink or menu. Then there are the many book clubs, which, because reading a book as leisure takes time, normally assemble only monthly. In this case, however, this meeting is the capstone of the reading process as it has unfolded over the preceding weeks.

Seasonal Frame

Seasonal requirements blend with annual events, which, though not usually linked to a particular season, are known for taking place on a yearly basis. In the domain of leisure, such occurrences are legion: annual general meetings of organizations, annual commercial sales (for those who seek pleasure through shopping), annual playoffs in sport, annual holidays, annual arts festivals and concerts, annual community events, and so on. Again, these affairs, however agreeable, count for comparatively little in a retiree's overall leisure lifestyle. Nonetheless, in harmony with most of the monthly activities, they do contribute to that lifestyle, becoming a noticeable element in it at a certain time of the year.

By contrast, a multitude of leisure activities are directly related to the four seasons, either through their dependence on certain climatic conditions or through their place in the calendar as it encompasses the seasons. We have already observed that many of the outbacker activities are seasonal in the climatic sense. Some of the events and festivals mentioned in the preceding paragraph are, in effect, climatically seasonal, as are events such as lilac festivals (spring), ice-sculpting contests (winter), and pumpkin festivals (fall). Then there are the summer camps offered in the fine arts.[10] Nevertheless, many other kinds of leisure are needed to carry participants in these activities through a full year of free time in the amount available to a full-time retiree.

The calendar season presents a different set of requirements in work and leisure. Thus, seasons in the fine arts typically run from September through the following May or so. Courses in adult education are often offered according to academic term, frequently labeled as fall, winter, spring, or summer. Yet these titles rarely correspond accurately with the climatic season and seldom have anything to do with its properties. As a third example, consider summer programming on television, which for many years has been widely panned as boring. The long-held belief is that at this time viewer interest mostly lies elsewhere—hence the usual offering of reruns, reality programs, and other filler.

Seasonal requirements do make a difference in the leisure lifestyle, especially those directly related to a climatic season or to a calendar season. Knowing them helps people plan their leisure lifestyle so that they maximize the benefit they gain from it. Being aware of seasonal requirements will, for example, enable a retiree keen on traveling but equally passionate about attending concerts of the local symphony orchestra to plan well in advance. This person must settle on travel and performance dates that harmonize with each other. This is no mean feat when some of the most interesting among the latter clash with some of the most interesting among the former (as scheduled in guided tours).

Volunteering

Volunteering as a leisure activity—remember, it may be serious, casual, or project based—fits every previously mentioned temporal frame. A challenge for all volunteers whose services are valued by the organization that has engaged them and the targets of their volunteering is, when they have had enough of it, to learn how to refuse further requests to volunteer—to learn how to say "No." As volunteering is needed in all temporal frames, and because demand for their generosity is huge, they are subject to requests for help, whatever the frame. Thus, when the volunteer cannot say no to these appeals, burnout becomes a real possibility.[11]

SOCIAL FRAME OF RETIREMENT LEISURE

A key part of your leisure lifestyle is the company you keep while living it. When one's leisure is solitary, this is obviously no problem whatsoever. But when other people are involved, their company can either sweeten or sour the leisure experience. Maximizing the first and minimizing the second will take some planning.

For retirees, some or all of whose leisure is enjoyed with family, there is the distinct possibility that it will be, on the whole, both bitter and sweet. So, grandchildren can be a joy to be with in such casual activities as exploring in the outback, opening gifts, and swinging in a park. But their boisterousness and exuberance can be detrimental to thought-provoking serious family activities like a political discussion, game of chess, or intricate recounting of an important event. Further, older retirees may become frustrated with their own waning physical ability to keep up with youth in some activities. Better to select certain family members with whom to engage in particular serious leisure activities in places where such distractions are improbable. That is, hold the political discussion in a bar or coffee house, or schedule an evening of chess at your own home (with no children invited).

To the extent that leisure is undertaken with older family members (i.e., late adolescents and beyond) and leads to a richly positive experience, the rewards can be powerful. Joining a strong, deeply felt family bond to the many rewards of a serious leisure activity can produce a set, possibly a long set, of experiences like none other. Even casual and project-based leisure can generate such bonding, though these kinds of activities lack the added dimension of passion that inheres in serious leisure.

Of course, this level of emotional intimacy, joined with serious leisure, is also possible with close friends. But that level declines when the leisure partner(s) is a more distant friend or a mere acquaintance. Nevertheless, collective leisure requires the participation of other people. So, distant friends and acquaintances may well be better than no partners at all, especially when the individual is greatly attached to a serious leisure activity and therefore most eager to engage in it. How well Skype and similar communication inventions can surmount the barrier of distance is yet to be scientifically determined. They must be in many ways, however, an improvement over the postal letter, e-mail message, and video e-mail attachment.

What about strangers in your collective leisure? This is certainly possible. Jazz musicians playing at a public jam session may well be performing with people they have never met. How many golfers have had a stranger join their threesome to bring it to the course-required foursome? Online interactions in gaming, discussion forums, and social media routinely introduce users to people they've never met before. Furthermore, strangers, some of them new arrivals to the community, are common in many urban leisure clubs and societies. Although the positive emotional attachment that accrues to family and friends is not there with strangers, the latter may introduce some welcome new ideas. Moreover, they may eventually become friends. They may also bring some needed skills, knowledge, and experience.

In fact, the chance to meet strangers can be one of the attractions of the townie and traveler lifestyles. And part of this attraction may be that we can preserve a degree of anonymity in their company. The strangers do not know us and we do not know them. And that may be just fine for all concerned. In this respect volunteering is, on the whole, probably the area of leisure in which the chance of meeting and working with strangers is greatest.

In sum, as you plan your retirement leisure lifestyle, ask yourself how closely attached you want to be with others in your collective activities. In answering this question, remember that everyone in those activities shares an interest in them. Even among strangers, there is some important and respected common ground.

CONCLUSION

The most effective, exciting, and appealing leisure lifestyles must be planned and maintained, ideally by the participant. This book's foremost contribution to reaching this goal is to aid your planning. To this end, it helps to be familiar with the wide range of serious, casual, and project-based leisure activities and to have identified those you would like to pursue in retirement. The combination selected will, when engaged in, generate one or two of the lifestyles just described. It is important to remember that there are far more interesting leisure activities than any person can possibly pursue and that most people can possibly afford. Choices must be made, a process facilitated by attending to the principles of positive simplicity.

It is at the point of choosing activities and allocating time to pursuing them that selfishness can emerge. Leisure activities, especially the serious ones, have magnetic pull. This pull can be so strong that, at times, participants may be accused of being selfish in their use of time and perhaps money. These commodities are seen by those claiming selfishness as rightfully theirs. Such accusations may be denied by the participant thus "charged," leading most of the time to acrimonious argument. There is evidence of this in culture (e.g., Google "golf widow," "baseball widow," "theater widow") and in research, both showing that relationships can be severely strained by leisure selfishness.[12]

Such contretemps severely reduce the positiveness that is otherwise the hallmark of leisure. Planning well for leisure in retirement includes keeping selfishness at bay. One route to this goal is to include as much as possible those who would be adversely affected by an overly strong commitment to a particular activity. So get them hooked on traveling, collecting, hiking, bridge, or whatever your passion. If they have little interest in it, perhaps there is a parallel activity that appeals. She loves to hike; he has no taste for it, but he does love to assemble her photos from the outback into slide shows or posting them online. He loves to travel; her medical conditions prevent this, but she reads voraciously on the regions he visits, thereby being able to supply him with a rich historical, cultural, and geographical background of them.

Good leisure is too precious to let slip from one's grasp. Plan well, and you will find the type of leisure that is most rewarding and satisfying to you.

Appendix

Nature Challenge Activities (Hobbyist/Amateur)

Air

- Skydiving
- Paragliding
- Hang gliding
- Microlighting
- Ballooning
- Gliding
- Aeronautics (planes)
- Base jumping
- Snowkiting, kitesurfing, kiteboarding

Water

- Boating (including jet/power boating)
- Sailing
- Surfing
- Windsurfing
- Lake canoeing/kayaking
- Sea kayaking
- Whitewater kayaking/canoeing
- Scuba diving

- Free diving (breath-hold diving/apnea)
- Swimming (long distance)
- Waterskiing, wakeboarding
- Jet skiing
- Rafting
- Rowing (long distance, sport)

Land

- Rock climbing/ice climbing (cross-reference ice/snow)
- Mountaineering
- Hiking
- Scrambling
- Wilderness camping and multiday hiking
- Canyoning/canyoneering
- Caving
- Mountain biking
- Orienteering/geocaching
- Mountain running
- Volunteering (conservation and/or activity related—for example, search and rescue, maintaining trails, invasive species eradication, guiding, interpretation)
- Motocross/4x4
- Beach auto and motorcycle racing
- Horseback riding (wilderness)

Flora and Fauna

- Wildlife/nature photography
- Bird watching
- Fishing
- Hunting
- Trapping
- Gathering wild plant foods (mushrooming)
- Collecting natural objects (shells, leaves, rocks, etc.)
- Natural science activities, including amateur ornithology, astronomy, botany, entomology, meteorology, and mineralogy

Ice and/or Snow

- Skiing (downhill, cross-country, backcountry)
- Snowboarding
- Snowshoeing
- Snowmobiling
- Skating
- Sledding

Notes

1. WHAT'S AT STAKE IN RETIREMENT?

1. For example, Julian Beltrame writes that more than 60 percent of Canadians have no company-based pension plan. Moreover, today's low interest rates on safe government bonds may be too low to keep up with inflation. (Julian Beltrame, "Retirees Face Dramatic Drop in Standard of Living," *Calgary Herald*, July 1, 2012, F1.) In the United States, many employees with public-sector pension plans face substantial reductions in benefits, as well as an increased age at which the benefits will be available ("Burning Fast," *Economist*, June 21, 2012, 34.

2. Duane Elgin, *Voluntary Simplicity: Toward a Way of Life That Is Outwardly Simple, Inwardly Rich*, 2nd revised edition (New York: William Morrow, 2010).

3. BlackRock, Inc. is an investment firm. See www2.blackrock.com/content/groups/global/documents/literature/blk_dc_survey.pdf (accessed May 28, 2012). See also the following editorial: "The Road to Retirement," *New York Times*, September 15, 2012, www.nytimes.com/2012/09/16/opinion/sunday/the-road-to-retirement.html (accessed September 16, 2012).

4. Max Kaplan, *Leisure in America: A Social Inquiry* (New York: John Wiley, 1960), 22–25.

5. Robert A. Stebbins, *Personal Decisions in the Public Square: Beyond Problem Solving into a Positive Sociology* (New Brunswick, NJ: Transaction, 2009).

6. "The Ironing Lady," *Economist*, April 21, 2012, 90.

7. Robert A. Stebbins, *Leisure and Consumption: Common Ground, Separate Worlds* (New York: Palgrave Macmillan, 2009).

8. See, for example, Daniel T. Cook, "Leisure and Consumption," in *A Handbook of Leisure Studies*, ed. Chris Rojek, Susan M. Shaw, and A. J. Veal (New York: Palgrave Macmillan, 2006), 304–16; Mathew McDonald, Stephen Wearing, and Jess Ponting, "Narcissism and Neo-Liberalism: Work, Leisure, and Alienation in an Era of Consumption," *Loisir et Société/Society and Leisure* 30 (2007): 489–510.

9. The three hobbies studied were kayaking, snowboarding, and mountain climbing. See Robert A. Stebbins, *Challenging Mountain Nature: Risk, Motive, and Lifestyle in Three Hobbyist Sports* (Calgary, AB: Detselig, 2005) (also available at www.seriousleisure.net/digital-library.html Library).

2. LEISURE FOR RETIREES

1. Amanda Stephenson, "Many Older Canadians Rethinking Retirement," *Calgary Herald*, May 30, 2012, E1.
2. Presented here as most recently set out in Robert A. Stebbins, *The Idea of Leisure: First Principles* (New Brunswick, NJ: Transaction, 2012).
3. Robert A. Stebbins, "Serious Leisure: A Conceptual Statement," *Pacific Sociological Review* 25 (1982): 251–72.
4. David Horton Smith, Robert A. Stebbins, and Michael Dover, *A Dictionary of Nonprofit Terms and Concepts* (Bloomington: Indiana University Press, 2006), 239–40.
5. Robert A. Stebbins, "Volunteering: A Serious Leisure Perspective." *Nonprofit and Voluntary Action Quarterly* 25 (1996): 211–24.
6. Robert A. Stebbins, *Amateurs: On the Margin between Work and Leisure* (Beverly Hills, CA: Sage, 1979); Robert A. Stebbins, *Canadian Football: A View from the Helmet* (reprinted ed.) (Toronto, ON: Canadian Scholars Press, 1993).
7. Robert A. Stebbins, "Fun, Enjoyable, Satisfying, Fulfilling: Describing Positive Leisure Experience," *Leisure Studies Association Newsletter* 69 (November 2004): 8–11 (also available at www.seriousleisure.net/digital-library, "Leisure Reflections No. 7").
8. Mihalyi Csikszentmihalyi, *Flow: The Psychology of Optimal Experience* (New York: Harper & Row, 1990).
9. Robert A. Stebbins, *Challenging Mountain Nature: Risk, Motive, and Lifestyle in Three Hobbyist Sports* (Calgary, AB: Detselig, 2005) (also available at www.seriousleisure.net/digital-library).
10. Robert A. Stebbins, *Amateurs, Professionals, and Serious Leisure* (Montreal, QC/Kingston, ON: McGill-Queen's University Press, 1992), 22.
11. Robert A. Stebbins, *Between Work and Leisure: The Common Ground of Two Separate Worlds* (New Brunswick, NJ: Transaction Publishers, 2004), 9.
12. Stebbins, "Serious Leisure: A Conceptual Statement."
13. Robert A. Stebbins, "Pleasurable Aerobic Activity: A Type of Casual Leisure with Salubrious Implications," *World Leisure Journal* 46 (2004): 55–58.
14. See home page at www.gthhh.com.
15. "Up off the Couch," *Economist*, October 22, 2005, 35.
16. Jennifer Gerson, "Video Games Keep Kids Fit," *Calgary Herald*, December 8, 2010, B1.
17. Robert A. Stebbins, *Serious Leisure: A Perspective for Our Time* (New Brunswick, NJ: Transaction, 2007), 41–43.
18. Robert A. Stebbins, *Exploratory Research in the Social Sciences* (Thousand Oaks, CA: Sage, 2001).
19. *New World Encyclopedia*, "Edutainment," www.newworldencyclopedia.org/entry/Edutainment (accessed March 3, 2012).
20. Susan L. Hutchinson and Douglas A. Kleiber, "Gifts of the Ordinary: Casual Leisure's Contributions to Health and Well-Being," *World Leisure Journal* 47, no. 3 (2005): 2–16.
21. Stebbins, *Serious Leisure: A Conceptual Statement.*
22. Hutchinson and Kleiber, "Gifts of the Ordinary."
23. Ken Roberts, *Leisure in Contemporary Society* (Wallingford, UK: CABI Publishing, 1999), 9–13.
24. Alison Pedlar, "Community Development: What Does It Mean for Recreation and Leisure," *Journal of Applied Recreation Research* 21 (1996): 5–23; Leslie Ploch, "Community

Development in Action: A Case Study," *Journal of Community Development and Society* 7 (1976): 8.

25. Stebbins, "Volunteering."

26. Robert A. Stebbins, "Project-Based Leisure: Theoretical Neglect of a Common Use of Free Time," *Leisure Studies* 24 (2005): 1–11.

27. Robert A. Stebbins, *The Organizational Basis of Leisure Participation: A Motivational Exploration* (State College, PA: Venture Publishing, 2002).

28. Robert Dubin, *Central Life Interests: Creative Individualism in a Complex World* (New Brunswick, NJ: Transaction, 1992).

3. AMATEUR ACTIVITIES

1. Thomas Munro, "Four Hundred Arts and Types of Art," *Journal of Aesthetics and Art Criticism* 16 (1957): 44–65.

2. Roch Carrier, "What Price Culture?" *Financial Post*, October 28, 1995, 23.

3. Jay Coakley, *Sport in Society: Issues and Controversies*, 7th ed. (New York: McGraw-Hill, 2001), 20.

4. Amateur wrestling has no professional counterpart. What passes for professional wrestling is not sport at all, but rather popular theater.

5. This is not an attempt to liken amateur scientists to tradesmen. In everyday usage, these three terms are applied to any field where extensive knowledge and ability must be developed before independent practice is possible.

6. These three concepts are further discussed in Robert A. Stebbins, "Avocational Science: The Amateur Routine in Archaeology and Astronomy," *International Journal of Comparative Sociology* 21 (March–June 1980): 34–48.

7. All amateurs, apprentices included, are aware of the possibility of accidentally discovering something new. But even apprentices observe or do fieldwork chiefly for other reasons, realizing how rare such discoveries are.

8. Schools have been established for training professional performers in magic, clowning, stand-up comedy, and the various circus arts. Besides being for future professionals only, they are geographically inaccessible for the most part, located as they are in just two or three cities in all of North America.

4. HOBBIES

1. Allan D. Olmsted, "Collecting: Leisure, Investment, or Obsession?" *Journal of Social Behavior and Personality* 6 (1991): 287–306.

2. Robert P. Overs, *Guide to Avocational Activities* (Sussex, WI: Signpost Press, 1984).

3. Lee Davidson and Robert A. Stebbins, *Serious Leisure and Nature: Sustainable Consumption in the Outdoors* (Houndmills, Basingstoke, UK: Palgrave Macmillan, 2011).

4. According to About.com, most doll collectors are female, but some males do take an interest in this hobby. "Top 10 Doll Collecting Myths," *About.com*, 2012, http://collectdolls.about.com/od/beginnerscollectingguide/tp/dollmyths.htm (accessed September 17, 2012).

5. Robert A. Stebbins, *The Barbershop Singer: Inside the Social World of a Musical Hobby* (Toronto, ON: University of Toronto Press, 1996). Barbershop is in other ways atypical of the folk arts. For example, it has a complex organizational structure serving tens of thousands of members across the world.

6. To the extent that spelunkers engage in speleology, the scientific exploration and study of caves and other underground features, they are amateur scientists rather than hobbyist activity participants.

7. Davidson and Stebbins, *Serious Leisure in Nature*.

8. Davidson and Stebbins, *Serious Leisure in Nature*.

9. There is also no small number of body-centered activities of the casual leisure variety, among them walking, popular dance, and jogging, when defined as enjoyable.

10. *Ringette/Ringuette Canada*, 2012, www.ringette.ca/en-us/oursport/history (accessed September 15, 2012).

11. See www.boardgamegeek.com for a very comprehensive list.

12. See http://boardgames.about.com/od/cardgames/Card_Games.htm for a list.

13. Since some people make money playing bridge, it is fair to ask whether bridge should be classified as an amateur activity. But according to Janicemarie Holtz, the title "professional bridge player" is a misnomer. She argues that the people who play bridge for money do so as secretly paid partners in a leisure activity officially held to be strictly amateur. Janicemarie A. Holtz, "The 'Professional' Duplicate Bridge Player," *Urban Life* 4 (1975): 131–48.

14. See http://en.wikipedia.org/wiki/List_of_dice_games for a list of games depending largely or entirely on dice.

15. For a list, see www.goodreads.com/quizzes.

16. A huge list is available at http://en.wikipedia.org/wiki/Video_game_genres.

17. See http://index.rpg.net for its current list of 17,117 role-playing games.

18. Gary A. Fine, *Shared Fantasy: Role-Playing Games as Social Worlds* (Chicago: University of Chicago Press, 1983), 6.

19. There are many varieties of crosswords. See Puzzle Baron's Acrostics at www.acrostics.org for one popular variation.

20. Robert A. Stebbins, "The Liberal Arts Hobbies: A Neglected Subtype of Serious Leisure," *Loisir et Société/Society and Leisure* 16 (1994): 173–86; Robert A. Stebbins, *The Committed Reader: Reading for Utility, Pleasure, and Fulfillment in the Twenty-first Century* (Lanham, MD: Scarecrow Press, 2013), chapter 5. The intellectually oriented followers of politics who are committed to a certain political party or doctrine still spend a significant amount of time (and possibly money) informing themselves widely in this area. To be a hobbyist here, a person must pursue a broad knowledge and understanding; he or she must do more than merely proclaim, however fervently, such and such a political stripe.

21. David L. Altheide and Robert P. Snow, *Media Worlds in the Postjournalism Era* (Hawthorne, NY: Aldine de Gruyter, 1991), chap. 2.

22. Stebbins, *The Committed Reader*, 92.

23. See, for example, Robin D. Mittelstaedt, "Reenacting the American Civil War: A Unique Form of Serious Leisure for Adults," *World Leisure & Recreation* 37, no. 1 (1995): 23–27. Mittelstaedt describes his participants as amateurs, whereas I have classified them as hobbyists because they appear to have no professional counterpart.

24. An "infoshop" is either a storefront or a social center. It is a distribution point for political, subcultural, and arts information, typically in the form of books, magazines, stickers, and posters. Some infoshops also serve as meeting spaces and resource hubs for activist groups. These services are especially common in Western Europe and North America, though they do

operate in other parts of the world as well. See http://en.wikipedia.org/wiki/Hackerspace and http://en.wikipedia.org/wiki/Infoshop (accessed November 25, 2012).

25. Robert A. Stebbins, *The Franco-Calgarians: French Language, Leisure, and Linguistic Lifestyle in an Anglophone City* (Toronto, ON: University of Toronto Press, 1994).

5. VOLUNTEERING

1. Robert A. Stebbins, "Unpaid Work of Love: Defining the Work-Leisure Axis of Volunteering," *Leisure Studies* 31(2012): 4 (published online April 18, 2012, doi: 10.1080/02614367.2012.667822).

2. Coralie McCormack, Penny Cameron, Anne Campbell, and Kimberley Pollock, "I Want to Do More Than Just Cut the Sandwiches: Female Baby Boomers Seek Authentic Leisure in Retirement," *Annals of Leisure Research* 11 (2008): 145–67.

3. David H. Smith, Robert A. Stebbins, and Michael Dover, *A Dictionary of Nonprofit Terms and Concepts* (Bloomington: Indiana University Press, 2006).

4. Robert A. Stebbins, "A Leisure-Based, Theoretic Typology of Volunteers and Volunteering," *Leisure Studies Association Newsletter* 78 (November 2007): 9–12 (also available at www.seriousleisure.net/digital-library.html, "Leisure Reflections No. 16").

5. Mary K. Kouri, *Volunteerism and Older Adults* (Santa Barbara, CA: ABC-CLIO, 1990).

6. The National Association of Partners in Education may be viewed online at www.trademarkia.com/partners-in-education-75783556.html (accessed September 19, 2012).

7. Proliteracy, 2012, www.proliteracy.org (accessed September 19, 2012).

8. U.S. Forest Service, "About Volunteering," http://www.fs.usda.gov/main/volunteer/aboutvolunteering (accessed September 20, 2012).

9. For a lengthy list of interest groups in the United States, see .

10. "The Economist Intelligence Unit's Index of Democracy 2010," http://graphics.eiu.com/PDF/Democracy_Index_2010_web.pdf (accessed September 20, 2012).

11. For volunteering opportunities, see National Association Citizens on Patrol, www.nacop.org (accessed September 22, 2012).

12. Robert A. Stebbins, "Mentoring as a Leisure Activity: On the Informal World of Small-Scale Altruism," *World Leisure Journal* 48, no. 4 (2006): 3–10.

13. Katie Misener and her colleagues found that sports volunteering among older adults was an "extremely positive" experience. Katie Misener, Alison Doherty, and Shannon Hamm-Kerwin, "Learning from the Experiences of Older Adult Volunteers in Sport: A Serious Leisure Perspective," *Journal of Leisure Research* 42 (2010): 267–90.

6. LEISURE: CASUAL AND PROJECT BASED

1. Wayne Jonas, *Mosby's Dictionary of Complementary and Alternative Medicine* (Amsterdam: Elsevier/Mosby, 2005).

2. Robert A. Stebbins, "Contemplation as Leisure and Non-leisure," *Leisure Studies Association Newsletter* 73 (March 2006): 21–23 (also available at www.seriousleisure.net/digital-library.html, "Leisure Reflections No. 11").

3. George H. Lewis, "The Sociology of Popular Culture," *Current Sociology* 26 (Winter 1978): 1–160.

4. A minority of spectators are not present to experience casual leisure, but rather to pursue their serious leisure as accomplished athletes, performing artists, auto racers, and so on. Some are knowledgeable liberal hobbyists. They observe critically, knowing well the standards that guide the activities unfolding before them.

5. Logically, this is casual leisure for all participants, even though a few of them might be serious marksmen or baseball players and, consequently, hit the target more readily than the rest.

6. Robert A. Stebbins, *The Committed Reader: Reading for Utility, Pleasure and Fulfillment in the Twenty-first Century* (Lanham, MD: Scarecrow Press, 2013). See especially chapter 4.

7. The sale of e-books has risen dramatically, but physical books are still holding their own. David Streitfield, "Little Sign of an E-Book Price War," *New York Times*, December 23, 2012 (accessed February 17, 2012).

8. Stebbins, *The Committed Reader*, 66–67.

9. Source: http://dictionary.reference.com/browse/historical%20fiction (accessed March 2, 2012).

10. Alison Weir, *Mary Boleyn: The Mistress of Kings* (New York: Ballantine, 2011).

11. Taken from Quoteland.com. William Harvey was a seventeenth-century English physician.

12. Robert A. Stebbins, "Volunteering: A Serious Leisure Perspective," *Nonprofit and Voluntary Action Quarterly* 25 (1996): 211–24.

13. See http://www.canadianliving.com/crafts; http://www.hobbycraft.co.uk/; http://www.enasco.com/artsandcrafts/.

14. See http://www.spacecraftkits.com/Catalog.html; http://www.alibaba.com/showroom/wood-craft-assembly.html (accessed November 21, 2012).

15. See www.realadventures.com/g6441_cave-exploration.htm.

16. For Skits Galore!, see http://dragon.sleepdeprived.ca/songbook/skits.htm (accessed November 26, 2012). For iComedyTV, see www.icomedytv.com/comedy-scripts/funny/viewtype/humorous/33/comedy-skits.aspx (accessed November 26, 2012).

17. See www.answers.com/topic/pageant (accessed November 26, 2012).

18. For some people, such a date is not leisure but a disagreeable obligation, possibly even a frightening experience that circumstances have forced upon them.

19. See www.toastmasters.org/MainMenuCategories/FreeResources.aspx (accessed December 5, 2012).

20. Robert A. Stebbins, "Personal Memoirs, Project-Based Leisure and Therapeutic Recreation for Seniors," *Leisure Studies Association Newsletter* 88 (March 2011): 29–31 (also available at www.seriousleisure.net/digital-library.html, "Leisure Reflections No. 26").

21. Carol A. Adams, *I Remember It Well: Poetry Writing for Seniors* (Renfrew, ON: General Store Publishing House, 2007).

22. World Health Organization, *Active Aging: A Policy Framework* (Geneva: World Health Organization, 2002).

7. PLANNING A LEISURE LIFESTYLE

1. Michael E. Sobel. *Lifestyle and Social Structure: Concepts, Definitions, Analyses* (New York: Academic Press, 1981), 28.
2. Robert A. Stebbins. *The Committed Reader: Reading for Utility, Pleasure, and Fulfillment in the Twenty-first Century* (Lanham, MD: Scarecrow, 2013), 103.
3. Vic Murray and Yvonne Harrison, "Virtual Volunteering," in *Emerging Areas of Volunteering*, edited by Jeffrey L. Brudney, ARNOVA Occasional Paper Series, volume 1, no. 2 (Indianapolis, IN: Association for Research on Nonprofit Organizations and Voluntary Action, 2005), 31–33.
4. Dorothy A. Counts and David R. Counts, *Over the Next Hill: An Ethnography of RVing Seniors in North America* (Toronto: University of Toronto Press, 2005).
5. This may also be done online with cooperatives known for selling only products of decent quality. Still, by taking this approach, you miss your chance to directly discuss those products with knowledgeable salespeople. This may be done in the United States at Recreational Equipment Inc (REI), in Canada at Mountain Equipment Co-op (MEC), and in Britain at Outdoor Pursuit Co-operative.
6. Ray Oldenburg, *The Great Good Place: Cafés, Coffee Shops, Bookstores, Bars, Hair Salons and Other Hangouts of a Community* (Cambridge, MA: Da Capo, 1999). These third places are held by Oldenburg to be of tertiary importance *vis-à-vis* those of secondary and primary importance—namely, work and home, respectively.
7. Observed by folklorist Tómas V. Albertsson, personal communication, December 26, 2012.
8. Lee Davidson and Robert A. Stebbins, *Serious Leisure and Nature: Sustainable Consumption in the Outdoors* (Houndmills, Basingstoke, UK: Palgrave Macmillan, 2011).
9. Even travelers suffer with this necessity, perhaps most egregiously while flying long distances. I have yet to meet anyone who likes long air trips. Even doing so in the most pampered circumstances seems not to be enough to offset the discomforts of security, periods of waiting, baggage retrieval, sitting for long periods, and other disagreeableness.
10. These camps operate in summer, because their activities are often held outdoors and much more extracurricular leisure is possible during summer than in other seasons. That said, summer is also preferred for calendar reasons, chief among them the fact that school is not in session.
11. Robert A. Stebbins, *The Urban Francophone Volunteer: Searching for Personal Meaning and Community Growth in a Linguistic Minority* (New Scholars-New Visions in Canadian Studies quarterly monographs series, vol. 3, no. 2) (Seattle, WA: University of Washington, Canadian Studies Centre, 1998), 31.
12. Robert A. Stebbins, *Amateurs: On the Margin between Work and Leisure* (Beverly Hills, CA: Sage, 1979), 81–82, 221–22.

Bibliography and Resources

Adams, Carol A. *I Remember It Well: Poetry Writing for Seniors*. Renfrew, ON: General Store Publishing House, 2007.
Aging Horizons Bulletin: A Canadian Bimonthly Educational Webzine.www.AgingHorizons.com.
Altheide, David L., and Robert P. Snow. *Media Worlds in the Postjournalism Era*. Hawthorne, NY: Aldine de Gruyter, 1991.
Beltrame, Julian. "Retirees Face Dramatic Drop in Standard of Living." *Calgary Herald*, July 1, 2012, F1.
Brown, Caroline A., Frank A. McGuire, and Judith Voelkl. "The Link between Successful Aging and Serious Leisure." International Journal of Aging & Human Development 66 (2008): 73–95.
Carrier, Roch. "What Price Culture?" *Financial Post*, October 28, 1995, 23.
Coakley, Jay. *Sport in Society: Issues and Controversies*. 7th ed. New York: McGraw-Hill, 2001.
Cook, Daniel T. "Leisure and Consumption." In *A Handbook of Leisure Studies*, edited by Chris Rojek, Susan M. Shaw, and A. J. Veal, 304–16. New York: Palgrave Macmillan, 2006.
Counts, Dorothy A., and David R. Counts. *Over the Next Hill: An Ethnography of RVing Seniors in North America*. Toronto: University of Toronto Press, 2005.
Csikszentmihalyi, Mihalyi. *Flow: The Psychology of Optimal Experience*. New York: Harper & Row, 1990.
Davidson, Lee, and Robert A. Stebbins. *Serious Leisure and Nature: Sustainable Consumption in the Outdoors*. Houndmills, UK: Palgrave Macmillan, 2011.
De Koven, Bernie, Deepfun.com.http://deepfun.com/Funsmith.html.
Dubin, Robert. *Central Life Interests: Creative Individualism in a Complex World*. New Brunswick, NJ: Transaction, 1992.
Economist. "Up Off the Couch." October 22, 2005, 35.
———. "The Economist Intelligence Unit's Index of Democracy 2010." www.graphics.eiu.com/PDF/Democracy_Index_2010_web.pdf (accessed September, 20 2012).
———. "The Ironing Lady." April, 21, 2012, 90.
———. "Burning Fast." June, 21, 2012, 34.

Elgin, Duane. *Voluntary Simplicity: Toward a Way of Life That Is Outwardly Simple, Inwardly Rich*. 2nd revised edition. New York: William Morrow, 2010.

Fine, Gary A. *Shared Fantasy: Role-Playing Games as Social Worlds*. Chicago: University of Chicago Press, 1983.

Gerson, Jennifer. "Video Games Keep Kids Fit." *Calgary Herald*, December 8, 2010, B1.

Heo, Jinmoo, Robert A. Stebbins, Junhyoung Kim, and Inheok Lee. "Serious Leisure, Life Satisfaction, and Health of Older Adults." *Leisure Sciences* 35 (2013): 16–32.

Holtz, Janicemarie A. "The 'Professional' Duplicate Bridge Player." *Urban Life* 4 (1975): 131–48.

Hutchinson, Susan L., and Douglas A. Kleiber. "Gifts of the Ordinary: Casual Leisure's Contributions to Health and Well-Being." *World Leisure Journal* 47, no. 3 (2005): 2–16.

Jonas, Wayne. *Mosby's Dictionary of Complementary and Alternative Medicine*. Amsterdam: Elsevier/Mosby, 2005.

Kaplan, Max. *Leisure in America: A Social Inquiry*. New York: John Wiley, 1960.

Kouri, Mary K. *Volunteerism and Older Adults*. Santa Barbara, CA: ABC-CLIO, 1990.

Leitner, Michael, J., and Sara F. Leitner. *Leisure in Later Life*. 4th ed. Urbana, IL: Sagamore, 2012.

Lewis, George H. "The Sociology of Popular Culture." *Current Sociology* 26 (Winter 1978): 1–160.

McCormack, Coralie, Penny Cameron, Anne Campbell, and Kimberley Pollock. "I Want to Do More Than Just Cut the Sandwiches: Female Baby Boomers Seek Authentic Leisure in Retirement." *Annals of Leisure Research* 11 (2008): 145–67.

McDonald, Mathew, Stephen Wearing, and Jess Ponting. "Narcissism and Neo-Liberalism: Work, Leisure, and Alienation in an Era of Consumption." *Loisir et Société/Society and Leisure* 30 (2007): 489–510.

Misener, Katie, Alison Doherty, and Shannon Hamm-Kerwin. "Learning from the Experiences of Older Adult Volunteers in Sport: A Serious Leisure Perspective." *Journal of Leisure Research* 42 (2010): 267–90.

Mittelstaedt, Robin D. "Reenacting the American Civil War: A Unique Form of Serious Leisure for Adults." *World Leisure & Recreation* 37, no. 1 (1995): 23–27.

Munro, Thomas. "Four Hundred Arts and Types of Art." *Journal of Aesthetics and Art Criticism* 16 (1957): 44–65.

Murray, Vic, and Yvonne Harrison. "Virtual Volunteering." In *Emerging Areas of Volunteering* (ARNOVA Occasional Paper Series, volume 1, no. 2), edited by Jeffrey L. Brudney, 31–47. Indianapolis, IN: Association for Research on Nonprofit Organizations and Voluntary Action, 2005.

New World Encyclopedia. "Edutainment." http://www.newworldencyclopedia.org/entry/Edutainment (accessed March 3, 2012).

New York Times. Editorial, "The Road to Retirement." September 15, 2012. http://www.nytimes.com/2012/09/16/opinion/sunday/the-road-to-retirement.html (accessed September 16, 2012).

Oldenburg, Ray. *The Great Good Place: Cafés, Coffee Shops, Bookstores, Bars, Hair Salons and Other Hangouts of a Community*. Cambridge, MA: Da Capo, 1999.

Olmsted, Allan D. "Collecting: Leisure, Investment, or Obsession?" *Journal of Social Behavior and Personality* 6 (1991): 287–306.

Overs, Robert P. *Guide to Avocational Activities*. Sussex, WI: Signpost Press, 1984.

Pedlar, Alison. "Community Development: What Does It Mean for Recreation and Leisure." *Journal of Applied Recreation Research* 21 (1996): 5–23.

Ploch, Leslie. "Community Development in Action: A Case Study." *Journal of Community Development and Society* 7 (1976): 8.

Roberts, Ken. *Leisure in Contemporary Society*. Wallingford, UK: CABI Publishing, 1999.

Smith, David Horton, Robert A. Stebbins, and Michael Dover. *A Dictionary of Nonprofit Terms and Concepts*. Bloomington: Indiana University Press, 2006.

Sobel, Michael E. *Lifestyle and Social Structure: Concepts, Definitions, Analyses*. New York: Academic Press, 1981.

Stebbins, Robert A. *Amateurs: On the Margin between Work and Leisure*. Beverly Hills, CA: Sage, 1979.

———. "Avocational Science: The Amateur Routine in Archaeology and Astronomy." *International Journal of Comparative Sociology* 21 (March–June 1980): 34–48.

———. "Serious Leisure: A Conceptual Statement." *Pacific Sociological Review* 25 (1982): 251–72.

———. *Amateurs, Professionals, and Serious Leisure*. Montreal, QC/Kingston, ON: McGill-Queen's University Press, 1992.

———. *Canadian Football: A View from the Helmet* (reprinted ed.). Toronto, ON: Canadian Scholars Press, 1993.

———. "The Liberal Arts Hobbies: A Neglected Subtype of Serious Leisure." *Loisir et Société/Society and Leisure* 16 (1994): 173–86.

———. *The Franco-Calgarians: French Language, Leisure, and Linguistic Lifestyle in an Anglophone City*. Toronto, ON: University of Toronto Press, 1994.

———. "Volunteering: A Serious Leisure Perspective." *Nonprofit and Voluntary Action Quarterly* 25 (1996): 211–24.

———. *The Barbershop Singer: Inside the Social World of a Musical Hobby*. Toronto, ON: University of Toronto Press, 1996.

———. *The Urban Francophone Volunteer: Searching for Personal Meaning and Community Growth in a Linguistic Minority* (Vol. 3, no. 2, New Scholars-New Visions in Canadian Studies quarterly monographs series). Seattle: University of Washington, Canadian Studies Centre, 1998.

———. *Exploratory Research in the Social Sciences*. Thousand Oaks, CA: Sage, 2001.

———. *The Organizational Basis of Leisure Participation: A Motivational Exploration*. State College, PA: Venture Publishing, 2002.

———. "Pleasurable Aerobic Activity: A Type of Casual Leisure with Salubrious Implications." *World Leisure Journal* 46 (2004): 55–58.

———. "Fun, Enjoyable, Satisfying, Fulfilling: Describing Positive Leisure Experience." *Leisure Studies Association Newsletter* 69 (November 2004): 8–11 (also available at www.seriousleisure.net/digital-library.html, "Leisure Reflections No. 7").

———. *Between Work and Leisure: The Common Ground of Two Separate Worlds*. New Brunswick, NJ: Transaction Publishers, 2004.

———. *Challenging Mountain Nature: Risk, Motive, and Lifestyle in Three Hobbyist Sports*. Calgary, AB: Detselig, 2005 (also available at www.seriousleisure.net/digital-library.html).

———. "Project-Based Leisure: Theoretical Neglect of a Common Use of Free Time." *Leisure Studies* 24 (2005): 1–11.

———. "Mentoring as a Leisure Activity: On the Informal World of Small-Scale Altruism." *World Leisure Journal* 48, no. 4 (2006): 3–10.

———. "Contemplation as Leisure and Non-leisure." *Leisure Studies Association Newsletter* 73 (March 2006): 21–23 (also available at www.seriousleisure.net/digital-library.html, "Leisure Reflections No. 11").

———. *Serious Leisure: A Perspective for Our Time*. New Brunswick, NJ: Transaction, 2007.

———. "A Leisure-Based, Theoretic Typology of Volunteers and Volunteering." *Leisure Studies Association Newsletter* 78 (November 2007): 9–12 (also available at www.seriousleisure.net/digital-library.html, "Leisure Reflections No. 16").

———. *Personal Decisions in the Public Square: Beyond Problem Solving into a Positive Sociology*. New Brunswick, NJ: Transaction, 2009.

———. *Leisure and Consumption: Common Ground, Separate Worlds*. New York: Palgrave Macmillan, 2009.

———. "Personal Memoirs, Project-Based Leisure and Therapeutic Recreation for Seniors." *Leisure Studies Association Newsletter* 88 (March 2011): 29–31 (also available at www.seriousleisure.net/digital-library.html, "Leisure Reflections No. 26").

———. *The Idea of Leisure: First Principles*. New Brunswick, NJ: Transaction, 2012.

———. "Unpaid Work of Love: Defining the Work-Leisure Axis of Volunteering." *Leisure Studies* 31 (2012): 4 (published online April 18, 2012, doi: 10.1080/02614367.2012.667822).

———. "Interview: Serious Leisure: The Ticket to a Fulfilling Retirement." *Aging Horizons Bulletin: A Canadian Bimonthly Educational Webzine* (July–August 2012), www.AgingHorizons.com (accessed March 9, 2013).

———. *The Committed Reader: Reading for Utility, Pleasure, and Fulfillment in the Twenty-First Century*. Lanham, MD: Scarecrow Press, 2013.

Stephenson, Amanda. "Many Older Canadians Rethinking Retirement." *Calgary Herald*, May 30, 2012, E1.

Streitfield, David. "Little Sign of an E-Book Price War." *New York Times*, December 23, 2012, www.nytimes.com (accessed February 17, 2012).

Weir, Alison. *Mary Boleyn: The Mistress of Kings*. New York: Ballantine, 2011.

World Health Organization. *Active Ageing: A Policy Framework*. Geneva: World Health Organization, 2002.

Index

active aging, 127
activity participation, 73–78; as body-centered activities, 76, 156n9; careers in, 77; definition of, 73; as folk art, 73–74, 156n5; as nature activities, 74–76, 138, 159n5; social worlds of, 77–78
amateur activities, 35–60; compared with other serious pursuits, 61; getting started in, 52–58; nature challenge, 149–151; positive simplicity for, 59–60; in townie lifestyle, 135–136. *See also* amateurs; fine and entertainment arts; science; sport
amateurs, 17; and professionals, 47–48, 51–52, 156n13, 156n23; types of in science, 48–49. *See also* amateur activities
art. *See* fine and entertainment art

de Balzac, Honoré, 35
boredom, 27

Casals, Pablo, xi
casual leisure, 15, 23–29, 111–119, 158n5; and active aging, 127; benefits of, 25–27; costs of, 27–29; definition of, 15, 23; as hedonism, 24–25; at home, 132–133; lifestyle in, 130; in outbacker lifestyle, 139; in townie lifestyle, 137; types of, 23–24, 111–119

central life interest, 27, 30
collecting, 63–68, 155n4; careers in, 66–67; casual, 63; and commercial dealers, 63, 67; gathering vs., 65; social world of, 67–68; types of, 64–66
consumption, 9–11; compared with leisure, 9
continuing education, 142, 144; in the arts, 53, 54, 55–56; in hobbies, 62, 88, 89, 90, 91–92; in project-based leisure, 121, 122; in sport, 57
Csikszentmihalyi, Mihalyi, 20–21

Daniels, Christopher, 25
devotee work, 15, 21–23; criteria for, 22–23; in townie lifestyle, 137; and traveler lifestyle, 134; types of, 21–22. *See also* serious pursuits
Dubin, Robert, 30

edutainment, 25, 115–117; fulfillment available in, 116–117
Elgin, Duane, 5, 8
entertainment, 113–115
entertainment arts. *See* fine and entertainment arts

Fine, Gary, 80
fine and entertainment arts, 36–43; as art, 36–37, 132; careers in, 41; effort and routine in, 40–41; physical limitations

in, 42; social worlds of, 42–43; training in, 41–42, 155n8; types of, 37–40; work in, 40
fulfillment (self), 15, 19; failure to find, 11, 35; and nonwork obligation, 8; vs. pleasure and enjoyment, 24–25; and positive simplicity, 6, 59; in project-based leisure, 29, 32; rewards of the serious pursuits and, 18–19, 20; vs. satisfaction, 19, 24–25, 95, 108; in serious leisure, 10, 43, 56, 60, 71, 75, 112, 120

Gregg, Richard, 5
Gregory, Philippa, 116

Harvey, William, 117
Hazlitt, William, 129
hobbies, 61–93; accessibility of, 61–62; activity participation, 73–78; collecting, 63–68; getting started in, 87–92; liberal arts, 82–87; making and tinkering, 68–73; monetary return from, 62; nature challenge, 149–151; positive simplicity for, 92–93; sports, games, and contests as, 78–82; in townie lifestyle, 135–136. *See also* hobbyists
hobbyists, 17. *See also* hobbies
Hutchinson, Susan, 27

Kaplan, Max, 6
Kleiber, Douglas, 27
Kouri, Mary, 99

leisure, 13–34, 111–127; as activity, 9; consumption and, 9–11; with family and friends, 145; homebody, 132–133; lifestyle, 129–147; in part-time retirement, 140; with strangers, 145–146; types of, 14–15, 16. *See also* active aging
Lewis, George, 113
liberal arts hobbies, 82–87; belletristic reading in the, 86; buffs in the, 82, 86, 158n4; consumers and, 82; definition of, 82; democratic access to, 83–84; and knowledge for its own sake, 82–83; and profundity of knowledge, 83, 156n20; as projects, 121–122; reading as, 84–86; social worlds of the, 86–87; in traveler lifestyle, 134
lifestyle in retirement, ix, x, 129–147; definition of, 130; financial challenges of, 3–6; geographic basis of, 130; homebody, 131–133, 140; nature of, 130; outbacker, 137–139, 142; part-time retirement, 139–140; planning for, 129–147; positive simplicity in, 134–135, 139; selfishness in planning for, 146–147; shaping leisure, 60; social frame of, 144–146; temporal frames of, 141–144; townie, 135–137, 159n6; traveler, 133–135, 159n9; types of, 130–140. *See also* optimal leisure lifestyle

Magener, Rolf, 135
making and tinkering, 68–73; activities in, 68–71; as breeding, 68, 71; careers in, 72; democratic nature of, 72; as projects, 119–120; social world of, 72–73, 156n24
McCormack, Coralie, 97
Munro, Thomas, 36–37

nature challenge activities, 75, 149–151

obligation, 6, 158n18; and leisure, 8; nonwork, 6–9, 60; in part-time retirement, 140; and positiveness, 6; in project-based leisure, 29, 33–34; in volunteering, 96, 97
Oldenburg, Ray, 136
optimal leisure lifestyle, 8, 11, 15, 28, 79; definition of, 27; and project-based leisure, 31; temporal aspects of, 141
outdoor activities. *See* activity participation, as nature activities
Overs, Robert, 63, 64–65, 68

play (including dabbling), 23, 24, 46, 112, 139
pleasurable aerobic activity, 119
positiveness, ix; in leisure, 10, 15; and nonwork obligation, 6; selfishness and, 129, 147; in volunteering, 157n13
positive simplicity, xi, 5–6, 34; for amateur activities, 59–60; consumption and,

10–11, 34; definition of, 5; for hobbies, 92–93; in leisure at home, 133; in outbacker lifestyle, 139; self-fulfillment and, 6; in traveler lifestyle, 134–135; voluntary simplicity and, 5

project-based leisure, x, 15, 29–34, 119–127; as active aging, 127; definition of, 29; in part-time retirement, 140; positive simplicity in, 126–127; and serious leisure, 30; social worlds of, 125–126; types of, 31–34, 119–125

project-based leisure projects, 119–125; activity participation, 122–123; arts, 123–125, 132; do-it-yourself, 120; entertainment theater, 123–124; genealogy, 121; liberal arts, 121–122; making and tinkering, 119–120; as memoirs, 124–125; other kit assembly, 120; public speaking, 124; Renaissance man reading, 122; tourism, 121–122; volunteering, 122–123

relaxation, 112–113

retirement: active aging and, 127; financing, 3–6; opportunities in, 35; part-time, 139–140; planning for, 129–147; plans, 153n1; social frame for leisure in, 144–146; temporal frames for leisure in, 141–144

Roberts, Ken, 28

Schopenhauer, Arthur, 28

Schweitzer, Albert, 95

science, 48–52; amateur careers in, 51; amateur wings in, 49–50; armchair participants in, 48, 85; core amateur activities in, 50–51; in outbacker lifestyle, 138; professionals in, 48, 49, 51–52; social worlds of, 51–52; in townie lifestyle, 135; types of amateurs in, 48–49, 155n5

sensory stimulation, 117–118

serious leisure, x, 16–21; dabbling and, 112; definition of, 14; lifestyle in, 130; in outbacker lifestyle, 138. *See also* amateur activities; hobbies; serious pursuits; volunteering

serious leisure perspective, 15, 16, 30

serious pursuits, 15–23; as active aging, 127; definition of, 14–15; rewards, costs, and motivation of, 18–20; selfishness and, 146–147; sport as, 43, 132; thrills and flow in, 20–21. *See also* serious leisure; devotee work

Sobel, Michael, 130

sociable conversation, 117

sport, 43–48; careers in, 46–47; definition of, 43; elite amateur, 45, 47–48; as entertainment, 43–44; physical limitations in, 46–47; professional, 45, 47–48; as a serious pursuit, 43, 132; social worlds in, 47–48; training in, 46–47; types of, 44–45. *See also* sports, games, and contests

sports, games, and contests, 78–82; careers in, 81; individual sports, 78–79, 132; puzzles and mazes, 81, 132; social worlds of, 81–82; team sports, 78; types of games, 79–80, 132

starting a leisure activity, 52–58, 87–92; activity participation, 88–90; art, 55–56; collecting, 87; dance, 54; liberal arts hobbies, 91–92; literature, 56; making and tinkering, 88; music, 52–54; science, 58; sport (amateur), 56–58; sports, games, and contests (hobbyist), 90–91; theater, 54–55; volunteering, 108–109

temporal frames of retirement leisure, 141–144; daily, 141; monthly, 142–143; seasonal, 143–144, 159n10; and volunteering, 144; weekly, 142

Thoreau, Henry David, 61

tourism: in traveler lifestyle, 133–135. *See also* project-based leisure projects; hobbies, liberal arts

volunteers and volunteering, x, 17, 95–110; altruism and, 17, 96; career, 96–97, 107–108; casual, 23, 28, 96–97, 108, 118; definition of, 95, 96; as e-volunteering, 132; and getting started, 108–109; marginal, 98; nature of, 97–98; and positive simplicity, 110; and professionals, 97; project-based, 32–33, 122–123; remuneration of, 95;

scope of, 98–107; by sector in community, 99–107; self-interest and, 17, 96; temporal time frames and, 144; types of interest driving, 98

well-being, 5, 15, 27, 127
World Health Organization, 127

About the Author

Robert Stebbins, PhD, is faculty professor and professor emeritus at the University of Calgary. He is the author or editor of over forty books, including *The Committed Reader: Reading for Utility, Pleasure, and Fulfillment in the Twenty-first Century* (2013), *The Idea of Leisure: First Principles* (2012), and *Serious Leisure and Nature: Sustainable Consumption in the Outdoors* (2011, with Lee Davidson). Stebbins is an elected fellow of the Academy of Leisure Sciences (1996), Royal Society of Canada (1999), and World Leisure Academy (2010). He is also an elected member of Phi Beta Kappa, Epsilon of Minnesota at Macalester College (2011). The website for the serious leisure perspective, on which this book is based, is available at www.seriousleisure.net.